Guaranteed Steps
to Managing Stress

GUARANTEED STEPS TO

MANAGING

STRESS

ARNOLD BURRON/JERRY CREWS

Tyndale House Publishers, Inc.
Wheaton, Illinois

All Scriptures, unless otherwise noted, are from
The Living Bible. Scripture quotations marked
RSV are from *The Revised Standard Version* of
the Holy Bible, copyright 1946, 1952, 1971 by
Division of Christian Education of the National
Council of Churches of Christ in the United States
of America. Scripture quotations marked KJV are
from the *King James Version* of the Bible.
Scripture quotations marked NKJV are from the
New King James Version of the Bible, copyright
1982 by Thomas Nelson, Inc.

Second printing, June 1987

Library of Congress Catalog Card Number 86-50430
ISBN 0-8423-1249-8
Copyright 1986 by Arnold Burron and Jerry Crews
All rights reserved
Printed in the United States of America

"The spiritual man has insight into everything, and that bothers and baffles the man of the world, who can't understand him at all.

"How could he? For certainly he has never been one to know the Lord's thoughts, or to discuss them with him, or to move the hands of God by prayer. But, strange as it seems, we Christians actually do have within us a portion of the very thoughts and mind of Christ."

1 Corinthians 2:15, 16

Contents

Foreword

A worldwide audience of millions of people, perhaps
the largest audience ever to view a single event,
watched with undistracted attention every detail of the
funeral of President John F. Kennedy. One week later, a
twenty-seven-year-old army captain, the commander of
the ceremonial troops whose every movement the world
had scrutinized, collapsed and died.

The middle-aged wife of the owner of the motel where
Martin Luther King died of an assassin's bullet suffered
a stroke and died the next day.

A fifty-six-year-old man, ecstatic over scoring his first
hole-in-one, dropped dead while enjoying the
congratulations of his friends.

A seventy-five-year-old man, waiting to cash in a
winning $1,683 ticket on a $2 bet, collapsed and
died.[1,2]

A fifty-eight-year-old professor, who had given years of
faithful service to a university, was anticipating a
comfortable retirement. He suffered a crippling stroke
less than two hours after being informed that his
hoped-for retirement benefits were to be reduced
dramatically.

Almost any professional in the health and human services fields can easily recall situations in which people suffered physical or psychological trauma shortly after experiencing extreme stress, both positive and negative.

In *The Big Book* of Alcoholics Anonymous, the recovering alcoholic is warned to avoid too much anxiety *and* too much happiness. Either condition, the book cautions, can keep him from his main goal: sobriety.

Recovering alcoholics are urged to flee, both figuratively and literally if necessary, any potentially negative stressful situations. And euphoria—the feeling that no problem is insurmountable—is regarded with the same seriousness as negative situations. A euphoric individual is too happy to notice implicit danger, and he feels too much in control to react appropriately to explicit danger. This person convinces himself that "just one drink can't hurt," and he ends up slipping back into his old habits, becoming enslaved once again to alcoholism.

Centuries before *The Big Book* was ever written, the apostle Paul warned his followers of the dangers inherent in both sadness and euphoria. He recognized the threat these conditions posed in deterring the Christian from his ultimate goal of faith in Jesus Christ and life everlasting.

"Happiness or sadness or wealth," Paul declared in his Letter to the Corinthians, "should not keep anyone from doing God's work" (1 Corinthians 7:30). To allow this could ultimately lead to the loss of faith in Christ, which, in turn, would result in remorse, self-recrimination, and a life devoid of God's peace, joy, and serenity.

Most books on stress and its management acknowledge that virtually every stimulus encountered by a living organism becomes a stress stimulus. The complete absence of stress is recognized as death. *So stress itself does not constitute a problem.* In fact, mankind often creates artificial stressors—a roller coaster ride, the vicarious danger in a movie, participation in vigorous physical or mental challenges—to provide a respite from mundane, everyday tasks.

The problem of stress results when we respond to stress inappropriately. Inappropriate stress responses cause "distress," which the dictionary defines as "anguish of body or mind; that which causes suffering." A thesaurus would include "distress" as a synonym for "anxiety," "discomfiture," and "fearfulness."

All of these conditions are opposite to the peace, joy, and tranquility that God promises us in his Word, and that each Christian seeks for himself and his loved ones. Distress—the mismanagement of stress—is debilitating, defeating, and destructive. It works to prevent a person from becoming, as Paul says in Romans 5:2, "all that God has in mind for [him] to be."

But why a book on stress management from a Christian perspective? Because although much has been written about the management of stress through diet, exercise, relaxation techniques, psychotherapy, chemical treatment, and a host of other scientific and quasi-scientific methods, the authors firmly believe that unless a person follows God's instructions in responding to stress, no complete, lasting, satisfactory management of stress can occur.

Successful stress management, then, is the ability to use our God-given capabilities to respond confidently and optimistically to triumph or tragedy, through the power of the Holy Spirit. This ability is best summed up in the apostle Paul's declaration, "I can do all things through Christ, who strengthens me" (Philippians 4:13, NKJV).

Stress management programs which exclude the

guidance and wisdom of the Holy Spirit, and which elevate secular theory, will not result in a victorious life. Paul, in his Letter to the Colossians, warns against ignoring God in the problem-solving process:

"Don't let others spoil your faith and joy with their philosophies, their wrong and shallow answers based on men's thoughts and ideas, instead of on what Christ has said" (Colossians 2:8).

The light that makes possible a sharp, clear, and accurate focus on the subject of stress management is the light of God's Word. It is in this light that a Christian approach to stress management is unique to the field.

One
Does God Keep Stress Away from Faithful Christians?

Preaching That's Poison

A stunned group of normally lively and talkative adults shifted uncomfortably in awkward, embarrassed silence. Their eyes were riveted on the white-haired woman who addressed them. Her words, punctuated with sobs, the trembling of her hands, and the strain on her face revealed her despair. She absolutely could not cope with what she had just been told by a middle-aged Bible study classmate, forty years her junior.

"It's simple," he had blurted in response to her troubled confusion on why God had not heeded her fervent prayers, and why he had allowed her terminally ill son to die. "You didn't have enough faith."

And now, her hands feverishly twisting a shredded tissue, she reasserted to the whole group the steadfastness of her faith during her son's ordeal. But her testimony failed to penetrate the barricaded mind of the classmate who had brutally asserted his dogmatic opinion. Had the woman sufficiently obeyed and believed, he declared, her son would not have died.

One of the most destructive teachings to infect Christians in recent years is that of "health and wealth"

Christianity. Briefly, this teaching can be summed up like this:

"You do your job of obeying and living right,
God will do his job of treating you right.
You will then enjoy perfect health and lots of wealth."

A less reverential way to put it is: "You obey and God will pay."

And those who promote this notion rush to tell eager and ignorant Christians that God is guaranteed to reward a good attitude and true obedience with dollars, or pounds sterling, or yen, or marks . . . or whatever the coin of the realm is. Do what you are supposed to do and "claim your promises," and you will be able to chirp a jingle similar to this familiar old refrain:

"Early to bed,
And early to rise,
Makes a man healthy, wealthy, and wise."

Just a few word changes will make the jingle suitable for use as a summary of the pop theology of "health and wealth" Christianity:

"Always obey,
Often give praise,
And you will stay healthy and get a big raise."

Unfortunately, this teaching is enthusiastically asserted and eagerly embraced by well-meaning, Christ-loving believers of many denominations. After all, it promises nothing less than heaven on earth, or the complete absence of troubles, problems, and poverty.

However, this idea that faithful Christians can avoid

all stress—that God will keep them from all stressful situations—is not supported by God's Word. And it results in Christians who, because they think they can avoid all stress, fail to manage the stresses they do encounter. Then they become wrapped up in attributing the presence of stress to some deficiency in their faith, or some wrathful vengeance of God. Their peace and joy— even their faith in Christ—become endangered.

The Scriptures do *not* teach that God will help faithful Christians to avoid all stress.

The Scriptures *do* teach that God will help faithful Christians to manage all stress.

Consider just one of many Scripture texts which discuss stress avoidance and management: "The good man does not escape all troubles—he has them too. But the Lord helps him in each and every one" (Psalm 34:19, 20).

What Is Stress? Before we go any further, let's examine what stress really is. The verse from Psalm 34 refers to "troubles," or any condition that might cause a person anxiety, perplexity, confusion, or sorrow, or even threaten a person's faith. These troubles cause "distress," or "anguish of body or mind; suffering." In short, distress is the absence of the calming peace of God.

But troubles aren't the only source of distress. Many of Christ's parables (the Rich Man and the Poor Man, Lazarus, the Prodigal Son, the Rich Young Ruler, etc.) and many Old Testament accounts tell of people who found themselves wealthy or successful, yet who lost sight of the things of God. These accounts teach us that successes can be dangerous too; they, like troubles, can cause distress.

Stress, then, is anything that blurs our focus on Jesus Christ, and in the process causes us to lose the peace God has given us. A Christian approach to stress management teaches us to use God's Word and his

guidelines to avoid stress when it's possible, and
manage the stress—both positive and negative—that
we can't avoid.

Step One in Stress Management
The young man was exceptionally good-looking, and
wore the best in fashionable clothing. He looked
comfortable in the most formal attire, yet had the kind
of lean masculinity that made even work clothes look
good on him. He commanded the attention of women,
and exuded confidence and authority. An aura of
strength surrounded him, as though he not only had
his act together, but knew, without being arrogant, that
he had his act together.

The woman, on the other hand, did not have her act
together. Nevertheless, she was seductively alluring, the
kind of woman that unattractive men knew was out of
the reach of even their most creative fantasies. Her
elegant bearing rendered her jewelry and expensive
fashions superfluous; she would have been
overwhelmingly desirable even without them.

On this particular day, as on many others, she burned
with desire for the handsome young man. Initially, her
overtures had been subtle. Experience had taught her
that her allure was almost innate—a kind of animal
magnetism that drew attractive men to her. But the
young man seemed oblivious to her beauty, which only
increased her desire for him.

She became more and more aggressive in her pursuit
of his attention, until subtlety was no longer possible.
She gave way to blatant provocativeness, and then to
an explicit invitation for him to have sex with her. Even
his direct rebuff—invoking his God and his deep moral
convictions—did not deter her. Her desires were out of
control.

Each day she repeated her invitation, until he went
out of his way to avoid her. Her ego had been so

pampered by past successes, that now her ardor increased with each rejection until she was as consumed by the challenge to satisfy her need for conquest as she was to satiate her lust.

Then, one day, the house was empty. Her husband was safely engaged elsewhere; she and the handsome young foreigner were alone. "Sleep with me," she murmured, reaching to grasp his jacket. Immediately the young man tore himself away, leaving his jacket clutched in her hands. As he pulled free, the resolve she had so often seen in his eyes to resist her was replaced by a look of repugnance. Her pride could not endure his look of disgust, and her plan for retribution—a way to salvage her pride—came to her almost immediately: She would tell her husband this man had tried to rape her.

At this point, the story of Joseph and Potiphar's wife, and Potiphar's angry reaction, are easy to recognize. Less obvious, however, are the stresses which Joseph faced both before and after being falsely accused. He was faced with:

1. The stress of repeated attempts at seduction by his master's wife.
2. The stress of imagining that his master might hold him responsible for the wife's adulterous behavior.
3. The stress of gossip and rejection by jealous fellow servants who may have noticed the woman's interest in Joseph.
4. The stress of bitter accusations by a master he had loved and served faithfully.
5. The stress of coping with God's seeming indifference to his plight.
6. The stress of being punished, rather than rewarded, for his righteousness.

7. The stress of feeling anger toward Potiphar's wife.
8. The stress of complete rejection by his fellow servants after he was accused.
9. The stress of being reduced to utter degradation just when it seemed he was getting somewhere in his life.
10. The stress of recognizing the hopelessness of a future in prison.

Almost all of these stresses, some of which were agonizingly painful for Joseph, were unavoidable. Even though Joseph had obeyed God, he was unable to avoid troubles. God, however, helped Joseph to manage his stresses. For example, God helped Joseph ignore Potiphar's wife's initial temptations. God helped Joseph rebuff her invitation, and led Joseph to extricate himself from the situation by calling on God's perfection. Then he helped Joseph flee from the woman's literal grasp.

In the midst of these struggles, we can be sure that Joseph relied heavily on his faith in God. In fact, when we next hear of Joseph, we see a man who has emerged from what could have been life-destroying stresses with a positive attitude and strong faith in God's benevolence.

Yet, Joseph could have compounded his problems by getting caught up in several other stresses that were avoidable. Consider the following stresses which Joseph would have had to face had he disobeyed God:

1. The stress of guilt over disobeying God and violating his master's confidence.
2. The stress of the fear of God's wrath.
3. The stress of the fear of discovery.
4. The stress of having to lie and cover up his sin.
5. The stress of having to continue to sin, lest his

master's wife accuse him of rape and provide
credible evidence.

6. The stress of enduring and coping with
legitimate accusations and rejection by his fellow
servants.

7. The stress of increased demands by his master's
wife, and perhaps even her friends, for
adulterous activities.

Had Joseph yielded to temptation, the resulting
stresses might have cost him his faith in God, for the
more deeply we plunge into sin the more we avoid God
in an Adam-like attempt to hide our disobedience. In
addition, Joseph's sin would probably have been
discovered since Potiphar's wife would no doubt have
boasted of her conquest to someone. So Joseph would
have suffered the stresses of accusation, rejection, and
imprisonment, but to a much more acute degree
because he would have been guilty.

God makes one point very clear: The most basic step
in successful stress management is to avoid undesirable
stress whenever it's possible. For example, I would not
encounter the stress of guiding an ice-coated car
through the fierce assault of a November blizzard on
Interstate 70 on the high plains of Colorado if I heeded
the traveler's advisories from the National Weather
Service. This doesn't mean that I will never be assailed
by a storm; I might take all the precautions and exercise
all the prudence in the world, and still be trapped by
an unanticipated snowstorm swirling out of the
unpredictable Rockies. But while I might not be able to
avoid *all* storms, I can certainly avoid some of them.

This same basic concept is taught throughout the
Scriptures: While Christians can't avoid *all* troubles,
they can certainly avoid *some* of them. And since
troubles constitute stress, it follows that Christians can,

indeed, avoid some stress. For example, here are some stresses we can avoid, and Scriptures that tell how to avoid them:

Stress

Marital problems caused because one partner is not a believer.

Scripture

"Do not be teamed with those who do not love the Lord" (2 Corinthians 6:14).

Picking up the pieces after doing something on impulse.

"Don't act thoughtlessly, but try to find out and do whatever the Lord wants you to" (Ephesians 5:17).

Problems with rebellious and disobedient children.

"Call them all together . . . to hear the laws of God and learn his will, so that . . . your little children . . . will learn how to revere the Lord your God" (Deuteronomy 31:12, 13).

Unanticipated debt as a result of cosigning a friend's loan agreement.

"It is poor judgment to countersign another's note, to become responsible for his debts" (Proverbs 17:18).

Frustration from being unable to attain high status and attention of others.

"This should be your ambition, to live a quiet life, minding your own business and doing your own work" (1 Thessalonians 4:11).

Scriptural guidelines for minimizing negative stress are abundant, practical, and easy to find. When we learn to use God's Word in this way, we will discover that it really is a "lamp unto [our] feet and a light unto [our] path" (Psalm 119:105).

Summary
In this chapter we've looked at the following points:
1. Stress can be caused by either troubles or successes, and is anything that disrupts our peace of mind or blurs our focus on Jesus Christ.
2. The Bible teaches that while all stress can't be avoided, some stresses *are* avoidable.
3. The Bible teaches that God helps his children manage the stresses they encounter.

Two
The One Stress You Can't Avoid

The Death Run

Two A.M. It was too early for the impenetrable darkness
and the cut of the night wind to be challenged by a
rising sun. Intermittent sleet rattled like rice on paper as
it swirled through the trees and against the jagged rocks
which marked the frozen mountain trail. His dagger
had been diligently honed the night before—caressed,
almost, until it was shard-sharp, capable of piercing the
thoracic cavity and puncturing the heart with one quick
thrust. Involuntarily, even as he ran, his hand dropped
to his hip to check for his weapon. It was there, as he
knew it had to be, and he grimly realized that tonight,
for the first time in over a thousand nights, he could be
a victim.

His awakening, always abrupt and always at two
A.M., had been different this time. Even his deepest
sleep had provided no respite from the consciousness of
a dead feeling in his legs. They felt hollow, devoid of
strength. Sleep had been difficult, and he had tossed
fitfully. Finally, at the appointed hour, the ritual of his
thousand risings had pulled him from his bed. He had
dressed quickly, girded his dagger around his waist with
a coil of rope, and plunged into the bitter darkness, clad
only in what he called his "Death Robe."

He ran for two hours, stopping at least a dozen

times—not because of the pain which intensified with each jarring step, and not because of the darkness, but to pray. And his prayers, like the pain in his gaunt and tortured frame, were more intense on this night. Again his fingers brushed his hip to check for his dagger.

Two hours of running were behind him; eight miles of dirt, darkness, and bitter cold. But there were six more hours of running to go; seventeen more miles of what was now excruciating agony. Each measured tread of his heavily calloused feet jammed his hip sockets and brutalized his calf muscles, jarring his upper back and jolting his neck like repeated blows from a fist. Perspiration rolled down his face, even as the raw wind sliced through the robe into his upper body.

The fear that on this night he would not make it clutched at his throat. Unless he turned back, he thought, a cold and lonely death awaited him somewhere on the mountainside ahead. But he knew, with fanatical certainty, that he could not turn back. Nor could he accept help if he collapsed from exhaustion or injury. He had committed himself. He would succeed, or he would die.

He stopped again to pray, and there was anxiety in his resolve. His comfort was bittersweet—after all, he was suffering for God. And if he died, it would be for God. Rasping a quick end to his prayer, he resumed his ascent of the mountain with renewed perseverance. His chest heaved; his breath was stolen in hollow gasps, his bones seemed to fracture with each tortured step. Surely God, who had looked upon his battered body clawing its way up the side of this jagged mountain a thousand lonely nights before tonight, would be pleased.

Twelve hundred years ago a Buddhist priest named Saicho founded a sect knows as the Tendai sect, which today boasts about one million adherents throughout

Japan. On Mount Hiei, north of the ancient capital of Kyoto, a cluster of thirty-one buildings constitutes the Tendai monastery. This monastery is the point of origin for a ritual which has endured since the sixteenth century.

A few zealots among the sixty high priests and eighty monks who inhabit the monastery aspire to attain the sacerdotal title of "master," or "teacher." These chosen few must, over a seven-year period, complete a run around Mount Hiei one thousand times. The grueling run, which takes about eight hours to complete and which begins each morning at two, poses obstacles larger than those which loom on the rugged mountainside. No monk who begins the run may return to the monastery without completing the course, even if he suffers a serious injury. Nor may he ask anyone for help.

Bones broken by injury, or a will broken by the ordeal of the twenty-five mile run—complete with two hundred sixty stops for prayer along the way—must not cause a monk to fail. The run *must* be completed. Failure means death, for failure must result in suicide. To ensure this, each novitiate carries a dagger and a rope so that he can stab or hang himself, and a purse of money to enable passersby to provide for a funeral. Even the monks' attire attests to the deadly seriousness of the run; their robe is called a "Death Robe"— testimony to the novitiates' solemn commitment to the thousand-day ritual, which only sixty zealots have survived in over four hundred years. No one knows how many monks, in their fanatically suicidal pursuit of self-generated purity and righteousness, have taken their own lives or perished in their attempt to perform the death run.

In 1984, the Associated Press reported that one survivor of the ritual suffered through the Death Run not only one thousand times, but one thousand five

hundred times. The monk, Yusai Sakai, is regarded
as a living Buddha by Tendai followers. He also
was reported to have "spent nine days continuously
chanting the Lotus Sutra in the compounds of a small
temple . . . without food, without water, without sleep,
and without lying down to rest," a feat which doctors
assert would be a medical impossibility for average
humans to survive.

Despite what the adherents of Tendai might argue is
the purpose of this ritual, it seems clear that they
believe that self-generated and self-imposed suffering
creates a personal purity, or "worthiness." For some
perverse reason, this idea has been seductive and
alluring to mankind throughout the ages. The reverence
accorded to Yusai Sukai by the followers of Tendai
demonstrates a strong belief that self-immolation
somehow makes one holy, or that self-imposed
suffering is somehow pleasing to God.

So mankind rises at two A.M. He shivers in the biting
cold of the dead of night. He dons a "Death Robe." He
embraces both the tangible implements of suicide and
the intangible probability of self-destruction. He
masochistically brutalizes his body, smashing flesh and
bone against frozen dirt and jagged rock as he agonizes
his way along a life-claiming trail. He gasps his prayers
and groans his chants. And he does this a thousand
times.

Then, slowly and unavoidably, doubt intrudes: Was
the sacrifice sufficient? Could it be possible that a
thousand agonizing twenty-five mile nights of self-
torture are not sufficient to placate an implacable God?
And so an additional five hundred days of agony are
endured through the scorching heat of summer, the
howling winds of spring, and the bitter cold of autumn.

Each person, in his own way, runs his own "Death
Run" in a never-ending pursuit of self-righteousness.
Yet, in spite of agonizing efforts, there remains an
implacable God who might be insistent upon even

more sacrifice. And so remain the persistent questions: Have I done enough? What more can I do? How will I know when I've done enough?

Modern Man's Death Run. A cursory review of world-wide religious practices throughout the centuries reveals that barbaric and sadistic sacrifices to appease God have always been practiced. Mankind knew instinctively—because the Law of God was written in his heart—that the demands of a perfect God were severe. What was *not* known was how to satisfy this demanding God.

To the Aztecs of ancient times, the answer lay in an endless stream of human victims, offered up in barbaric sacrifice to their angry and ferocious god, Quetzalcoatl. For Hindu fakirs, the road to sanctification lay in crude self-denial, or in complete self-debasement. Other mullahs of mysticism preach that freedom from carnal thoughts, and the peace of mind such purity would bring, could be achieved by thinking about the seven orifices of the human body and the issues which they excrete.

A more direct route to pleasing God is pursued by the fanatical modern day disciples of Shi'ite Islam, who eagerly embrace the opportunity to court death. They believe one can earn immediate salvation by engaging in "jihad," or "holy war," against infidels of any stripe. This is why fanatical Shi'ites charge into massive, concentrated machine gun fire on the battlefields of the Middle East.

A practice begun in earlier centuries, which persists even today, is that of showing penance through self-flagellation—beating oneself with glass-embedded whips to the point of shredding one's skin to a bloody mess. Many considered this their avenue to personal piety and righteousness before God. Even the offering of long prayers and the performing of demeaning tasks have been used to "do penance."

Some Christians, who don't know any better, walk

around with long faces and somber expressions, taking care not to appear too happy lest God notice their happiness and mistake it for a lack of piety or insincere repentance. Still other well-meaning Christians find themselves in pursuit of endless "righteous" activities, hoping to "feel" forgiven, or to "feel" joy and peace.

And for those who have turned their backs on all religion, modern society still holds many roads to personal "purity" and self-righteousness. These include philanthropy, politics, environmentalism, pacifism, militarism, one-worldism, jingoism, and association with charitable causes. A tragically large number of people have fallen prey to drugs—to the beckoning of a chemical "nirvana" that promises to anesthetize them. They know, innately, that they must escape; but they don't know, explicitly, *what* it is they must escape *from*.

Where Does Stress Come In?
Now, what does all of this have to do with stress? Or, for that matter, what does it have to do with stress-management from a Christian perspective?

In each of the cases discussed, the individual—the Tendai monk, the Hindu fakir, the Shi'ite Muslim— responded to *the same stress stimulus*, regardless of the exact nature of his response. This same stress stimulus faces you and me, and every human being who ever lived! As the apostle Paul tells us:

"He will punish sin wherever it is found. He will punish the heathen when they sin, even though they never had God's written laws, for down in their hearts they know right from wrong. God's laws are written within them; their own conscience accuses them, or sometimes excuses them" (Romans 2:12-14).

So even "the heathen"—those who do not know the exact nature of God's law—have consciences that bear witness to a perfect and demanding God, and that accuse or excuse them in relation to the demands of this God. Therefore, the most significant and inescapable stress stimulus shared by everyone is, in a word, *guilt.*

It is intriguing that everyone must face and manage this basic, universal stress of innate guilt. But even more intriguing is the fact that, in our attempts to reduce or manage this stress, we often select responses which have a totally opposite effect to what we desire. Extreme self-sacrifice or punishment, rather than reducing our original guilt or stress, often cause additional emotional and physical stresses! Not only do we fail to manage the original stress, but we end up with more problems than we started out with!

We experience stress *mis*management because:

Our self-sacrifices often cause emotional and physical stress.

We *still* have the stress of our innate guilt.

We have added the stresses from our inadequate responses.

So we end up facing *more* stress than we started with!

The apostle Paul sums it up very succinctly:

"For the truth about God is known to them instinctively; God has put this knowledge in their hearts . . . And after awhile they began to think up silly ideas of what God was like and what he wanted them to do. The result was that their foolish minds became dark and confused" (Romans 1:19, 21).

Managing Guilt Stress with Religion. For centuries, religions have imposed additional stress upon their followers by the very methods they prescribed for alleviating guilt stress. All non-Christian religions—and even some Christian denominations—produce inner turmoil and a lack of peace on one basic question:

"How do I adequately respond to God's demands?"

This was the same question the crowds asked Jesus in John 6:28: "What should we do to satisfy God?" The responses of religions to this question have been as great in their variety as they are in their inadequacy. Arduous pilgrimages, rigorous rites of penance, scrupulous adherence to elaborate traditions, meticulously followed rituals, man-ordained sacrifices and offerings, and rigid asceticism have all been promoted as methods to "satisfy" God. The more elaborate, demeaning, and difficult the religious response, it seemed, the greater its value.

While some men experienced a measure of self-gratification through these practices, only a semblance of peace was ever attained. There was no point at which a man could declare, "Enough!" and know, with a peaceful heart, that no more self-abasement was necessary. No pilgrimage, self-denial, personal sacrifice, or demeaning suffering brought lasting peace, joy, tranquility, or serenity. Always there lurked God's incessant demand for "more."

So, regardless of the nature, duration, or intensity of what any man may do to satisfy God's demands for perfection, that man will only be brought to an acute awareness of the fact that he is not perfect. He has determined in his mind that some type of sacrifice is necessary, but his most sincere, anxious, and even reverential spiritual and physical grovelings will only result in his feeling inadequate and guilty. Therefore, *guilt stress will always remain with the man who seeks to manage it with self-sacrifice.*

Do Christians Suffer from Guilt Stress?

Guilt stress is a familiar burden to many Christians, even though God has taught us how to manage it. The total inability to feel spiritually "good" is felt by all of us as we attempt to respond to the stark reality of our spiritual inadequacy. John the Baptist was, perhaps, the first individual in the New Testament to fully comprehend his spiritual inadequacy. Though he was sought out and admired by the crowds of his day as a model of self-sacrifice, he said in Matthew 3:11, "I am not worthy even to carry his shoes," speaking of himself in relation to Christ. Simon Peter also came face-to-face with his deep spiritual poverty, declaring in a moment of insight, "Depart from me; for I am a sinful man, O Lord" (Luke 5:8, KJV).

All Christians have felt the guilt and anxiety of spiritual inadequacy. Consider the following remarks:

> "I know I don't have enough faith."
> "I really ought to be spending more time reading the Bible."
> "If I were really spiritual, I wouldn't have these thoughts."
> "She/he is so much closer to God than I am."
> "I know God expects more of me . . . I do fine until . . ."
> "I repented, but I did it again. I'll never change!"
> "I know I should (or shouldn't), but . . ."

For Christians, managing guilt stress is a daily battle. Satan constantly tries to burden us with the unbearable fact of our spiritual inadequacy. But giving in to guilt stress only leads to frantic attempts to "feel right" with God through some type of self-sacrifice. All too often, a service we perform which should be offered with joy, ends up causing us distress. Is there really any difference between the following:

1. A twenty-five mile run by a novitiate "master" or one dutifully-tithed portion of inheritance money?
2. Nine days of continuous and torturous chanting

or one year of burdensome and unenthusiastic Sunday school teaching?
3. Two hours of self-flagellation or X number of Sundays of church attendance?
4. Thirty days of fasting or one year of reluctant service as a church elder?
5. One hundred nights of sleeping on a cold floor or sporadic guilt-inspired readings of devotional books, or repeated recitations of books of penance?

Behaviors such as those listed above, by pagans and Christians alike, led Jesus to offer us a compassionate invitation: "Come to me, and I will give you rest—all of you who work so hard beneath a heavy yoke" (Matthew 11:28). Ignoring this invitation and relying on our own wisdom to fulfill the perfect demands of a perfect God will always result in more stress. However, if we use the Scriptures God has given us, we can understand what to do about the stress of spiritual inadequacy.

The Gospel message of what to do about spiritual guilt constitutes Step One in a successful stress management life-style. What Christians need to do about guilt stress—spiritual inadequacy—is this: nothing. Nothing at all!

God promises us complete freedom from guilt stress, and his demands for spiritual perfection have been perfectly met. The *only* guaranteed method of managing guilt stress is found in Jesus' response to the question of the crowds in John 6:28, 29, which we mentioned earlier. "What should we do to satisfy God?" they asked.

And Jesus replied: "'This is the will of God, that you believe in the one he has sent'" (John 6:29). This response appears again and again in Scripture.

"I say emphatically that anyone who listens to my message and believes in God who sent me has eternal life, and will never be damned for his sins, but has already passed out of death into life" (John 5:24).

"But now God has shown us a different way to heaven— not by 'being good enough' and trying to keep his laws, but by a new way . . . Now God says he will accept and acquit us—declare us 'not guilty'—if we trust Jesus Christ to take away our sins. And we can all be saved in this same way, by coming to Christ, no matter who we are or what we have been like. . . . Then what can we boast about doing, to earn our salvation? Nothing at all. Why? Because our acquittal is not based on our good deeds; it is based on what Christ has done and our faith in him" (Romans 3:21, 22, 27).

"For it is from God alone that you have your life through Christ Jesus. He showed us God's plan of salvation; he was the one who made us acceptable to God; he made us pure and holy and gave himself to purchase our salvation. As it says in the Scriptures, 'If anyone is going to boast, let him boast only of what the Lord has done'" (1 Corinthians 1:30, 31).

"His sacrifice frees us from the worry of having to obey the old rules, and makes us want to serve the living God" (Hebrews 9:14).

These Scriptures and many others clearly show that there is absolutely nothing that a Christian can do to manage the stress of imperfect spirituality. He must have faith in Christ. But God does not stop at the point of providing his children with the necessary knowledge which leads to peace of mind. He provides a step-by-step process by which we can actually experience this peace of mind.

Suppose we, like many other Christians, have wasted much of our opportunity to experience freedom from guilt because we've been busy worrying about whether we "have enough faith" or are "good Christians." Suddenly we're overwhelmingly persuaded by the Scriptures that we do not have to constantly justify ourselves—that Christ really has set us free. Now we know that the stress of spiritual inadequacy is behind us; we don't have to worry about it. But we have not *experienced* the freedom from guilt stress. We know we are free, but we don't *feel* free. In 2 Peter 1, God gives us the steps to experiencing this freedom:

Step 1: "*Do you want more and more of God's kindness and peace? Then learn to know him better and better. For as you know him better, he will give you, through his great power, everything you need for living a truly good life: He even shares his own glory and his own goodness with us! And by that same mighty power he has given us all the other rich and wonderful blessings he promised; for instance, the promise to save us from the lust and rottenness all around us, and to give us his own character*" (*vu 2-4*).

Step 2: "*But to obtain these gifts, you need more than faith; you must also work hard to be good, and even that is not enough*" (*u 5*).

Step 3: "*For then you must learn to know God better and discover what he wants you to do*" (*u 5*).

Step 4: "*Next, learn to put aside your own desires so that you will become patient and godly, gladly letting God have his way with you*" (*u 6*).

Step 5: "*This will make possible the next step, which is for you to enjoy other people and to like them, and finally you will grow to love them deeply*" (*u 7*).

Step 6: "*The more you go on in this way, the more you will grow strong spiritually and become fruitful and useful to our Lord Jesus Christ*" (*u 8*).

Following these steps allows us to both know and feel the freedom of managing the most basic stress in our lives—that of our imperfect spirituality.

Summary
No program of stress management that excludes the work of Jesus Christ in removing guilt stress (the stress of the inescapable knowledge of our spiritual inadequacy) can ever be completely successful. Since everyone experiences this stress at some time in their lives, it is vital to realize that we cannot manage it on our own. Responding to this guilt stress with frenzied attempts to satisfy unspiritual appetites or by trying to attain piety through self-sacrifice, will only increase the stress we experience.

God has provided us with the only perfect response to our imperfect spirituality: Jesus Christ. Successful stress management begins when we accept God's forgiveness through Christ, and follow the scriptural instructions we've been given. Then we will find absolute peace and freedom from guilt stress.

"Since we have been made right in God's sight by faith in his promises, we can have real peace with him because of what Jesus Christ our Lord has done for us" (Romans 5:1).

Three
The Deep Thought You Can't Escape

Goal-Driven or God-Led?
The Stress of Finding Your Life's Purpose

"Mid-life crisis," "male menopause," "the empty-nest syndrome," "middle-age crazy" . . . even before the publication of Gail Sheehy's landmark book, *Passages*, psychiatrists, psychologists, clergymen, and lay counselors were aware of puzzling changes in the behavior and perceptions of people who had weathered many of life's tempests. Without warning, erratic behaviors often erupted in previously stable people when they either approached middle age or achieved a major goal (such as landing a certain job, or attaining a promotion, degree, or long-awaited purchase). These erratic behaviors included abrupt changes in tastes in clothing, automobiles, or entertainment; sudden and extreme frustration with one's profession or occupation; revision or even abandonment of lifelong values; sleeplessness, crying spells, inexplicable anger or vehemence, and wild mood swings; and the frequent occurrence of feelings of futility, such as "What am I doing here?" "Why am I doing this job?" or "What am I accomplishing that makes any difference?"

Some of these changes in behavior can be attributed to physiological causes. But the explanation is not always that simple; a physiological cause is not always present.

A new perception of life emerged for one career-oriented person when he felt he had met his goals; success had been achieved and there was nothing left to strive for. Others went through changes when they realized that they would not, after all, be world-famous or make a fortune. Some older people developed a new perception of life when their children no longer seemed to need them. Younger people often found a new perception emerging with their last lingering look at their home town or college campus as they faced a new beginning. Sometimes these new perceptions emerged slowly, other times they were the startling results of the dramatic intrusion of accident or illness.

For Bill Morelli, now a dedicated Christian who lives in Denver, Colorado, a new perception began the day the door slammed behind him in solitary confinement at the state penitentiary in Canon City, Colorado. He was being confined after stabbing and critically wounding another inmate with a mop handle. His new perception of life, and his consequent acceptance of Christ, emerged tentatively, like a thin ray of light that peeped through a crack in the door of his dank, cramped cell, and filtered through the darkness of his angry soul.

But whether a person's life situations are mundane or, as in Bill Morelli's case, dramatic, the theme is constant: The emergence of a new perception of life begins with the undeniable and sometimes bitter awareness of one's own mortality; that, regardless of achievements, honors, status, family, wealth, or anything else, there would be an End. One must die. This realization becomes the catalyst for a soul-searching that often leads to an urgent desire for purpose in life; for something that will give some meaning to existence.

The thirst for purpose has afflicted even history's greatest heroes. Following Alexander the Great's last battle, at which his final viable opponent lay prostrate and defeated before him, it is said that Alexander, the ruler of all tribes and nations then known to the civilized world, wept. He wept because there were no more worlds left to conquer. In one sense, Alexander the Great had gained the whole world. But in the process, he lost even more; his purpose for living was gone.

The theme of mankind's search for meaning is dominant throughout history. The stress and anxiety which accompany this search are so urgent that they always forced a response. The mysterious pillars of Stonehenge and the pyramids of Egypt are evidence of ancient man's response to this search. The tragedy of the followers of Jim Jones and the derelict-strewn gutters of skid row in every major city in the world are today's evidence of mankind's failed search for meaning.

As with any other stress, Christians are not immune to the stress of the quest for meaningful lives. And, too often, the Christian's focus on a victorious death obscures the availability of a victorious life. Christians expend their energies pursuing the same meaningless goals which their progenitors pursued centuries before, with an equal emptiness of purpose.

Martin Luther, the great leader of the Reformation, rendered this observation on man's motivations at various stages of life: "In his early years, a young man seeks sex. In his thirties, money. And in his forties and beyond, power." Luther also passed judgment on the worth of the pursuit of these goals through words of his immortal hymn, *A Mighty Fortress Is Our God:*

"And take they our life,
fame, child and wife,
Let these all be gone,
They yet have nothing won.
The Kingdom ours remaineth!"

Viktor Frankl, the famous Jewish psychiatrist who survived the horrors of a Nazi concentration camp, thirsted desperately for a purpose for existence, even as he was drowning in a flood of adversity. In his commanding work, *Man's Search for Meaning,* Frankl painstakingly described his discernment that a man must have a purpose for living—else he would perish. Amidst the fetid corpses, staggered by the rancid stench of disease and decay, and crushed beneath the heel of his oppressors, Frankl desperately groped for meaning. He knew, instinctively, that without some purpose he would not survive. But survive he did, by grasping and tenaciously clinging to the idea that if suffering was all that was available to him, his purpose would be to suffer well.

When evangelist Billy Graham was asked why the Soviet Union allowed him a second visit in 1984, he responded, "Because the Russian people are asking philosophical questions such as, 'Why am I here?' and 'What's the purpose of my existence?'" This is strong evidence of the universality of the need for purpose. Sadly, the stress created by this need is equally universal—and it often results in an urgent, consuming anxiety. Many famous people, whose material needs have been met completely and who seemingly should be free from concern, have fallen victim to the anxiety of purposelessness.

In mid-1984, *Wired,* the sometimes lurid account of the life and times of John Belushi, captured the attention of the national media. Curious people around the world spent millions on this and other exposé-oriented "unauthorized biographies" and self-stroking autobiographies of famous people. More often than not, it was revealed that those who seemingly had everything, really had nothing at all.

Patricia Nolan, a writer for *Rolling Stone* magazine, chronicled the lives of celebrities who were on top of the world with fame, wealth, and unlimited opportunity but who ended up destroying themselves attempting to fill the voids which existed in their lives. Nolan quoted Dr. Jerry Reback, a psychiatrist who counseled chemically-dependent celebrities:

"Many self-destructive celebrities don't seem to care if they live or die. They'll do anything to destroy their bodies and their minds. Meanwhile, as they are taking drugs, they'll whine and complain about how rough life is for them, and the awful stresses they have to face every day."

Reback and Nolan provided additional details about celebrities who seemed to "have it made," but who obviously were overcome by their stresses:

- Elvis Presley—died of a drug overdose.
- Dennis Wilson of the Beach Boys, of whom it was said, "[It's] almost as if he had a death wish"— drowned while drunk.
- Freddie Prinz, comedian and TV star—dead of a self-inflicted gunshot wound.
- John Phillips and his daughter, actress MacKenzie Phillips—almost died of drug abuse. Said John, "I lived for cocaine—it became the most important thing in my life."
- George Carlin, comedian—suffered a series of drug-induced health problems. "All I lived for was my next snort of cocaine."
- William Holden, actor—bled to death while drunk.
- Janice Joplin, rock star—died of heroin overdose.
- Jimi Hendrix, rock star—died of drug overdose.
- Bela Lugosi, actor—died as a result of morphine addiction.

In most of these cases, as with Alexander the Great, there were no more worlds left to conquer. The tragic deaths of these people resulted from lives devoid of significance or purpose.

But it is not just the wealthy who suffer this anxiety

of purposelessness. Most of us, at one time or another, have had experiences similar to those described below:

"A foundation is a foundation," the frustrated woman said despairingly. She sat with her palms upward in a gesture of surrender. "A fundamental is a fundamental." She was in her fifteenth year as a college professor, and the enthusiasm with which students registered for her classes was an ironic contrast to her own desperate boredom after teaching the same course one hundred and twenty-six times.

"It doesn't matter whether I use lecture, discussion, or demonstration; a course in the basics is still a course in the basics. It's still the same old stuff. I can't change the basics of the subject just to escape my own boredom. It's driving me nuts. And to think," she murmured almost as an afterthought, "I'm not even close to retirement. What's the point of it all?"

The golf course was empty. It was a good time for thought. "People kind of look at me in awe when they hear what I do," the pilot said. "Like it's so glamorous. But there are times I'd like to show them what flying is all about. Like, you could take that bird and really soar!" he exclaimed. Watching his ball come to a bouncing halt on the green, he shook his head. "This is your captain speaking," he twanged nasally. "It's boring and cramped up here in the cabin. I've been where you're going at least a million times. Ground transportation is lousy, and I can't wait to get back and really fly in my single engine machine."

His companion smiled, amused at his friend's mimicry. "It doesn't matter who does what, Larry," he counseled. "I get just as tired interviewing people every day. The questions are always the same: 'What kinds of jobs have you done?' 'Why did you leave your last employer?' 'Are you willing to relocate?' 'What's the minimum salary you'd accept?' If I have to interview one more manager-type who has dirty nails and unshined shoes, I'll have you push me out of the cargo hatch over Topeka!"

The problem is common. It's a feeling that, after all is said and done, one's accomplishments don't amount to much in the "Grand Scheme of Things." Percy Bysshe Shelley, the great British poet, made this the theme of one of his poems, "Ozymandias." He hauntingly describes the futility of human vanity and the fleeting glory of achievement: A traveler wending his way across the sun-baked expanse of a vast and desolate desert discovers a relic of the past glory of a mighty and extinct civilization—the half-buried remnants of a monument to its king. "My name is Ozymandias, King of Kings" the time-worn inscription on the monument declares. "Look upon my works, ye Mighty, and despair!"

The eerie nothingness almost floats, wraithlike, from the page, as Shelley describes what the traveler sees:

"Nothing beside remains. Round the decay
Of that colossal wreck, boundless and bare
The lone and level sands stretch far away."

In Ecclesiastes 1:2, 3, 8-11, King Solomon—whose wisdom has been quoted for centuries—echoes Shelley's dirge of despair. We can all instinctively identify with the bitter truth of Solomon's words:

"Meaningless! Meaningless!"
Says the Teacher.
"Utterly meaningless!
Everything is meaningless."

What does man gain
From all his labor
At which he toils under the sun?

All things are wearisome,
More than one can say.

The eye never has enough of seeing,
Or the ear its fill of hearing.
What has been will be again,
What has been done will be done again.
There is nothing new under the sun.

Is there anything of which one can say,
"Look! This is something new"?
It was here already, long ago;
It was here before our time.

There is no remembrance of men of old,
And even those who are yet to come
will not be remembered by those who follow.

Unfortunately, the response to such words is often a flight into the nihilistic world of drugs, sex, and dropping out, or a fevered embracing of the seeming purposefulness of the cult movements. What is really needed is productive and redeeming introspection. But cynicism and despair, rather than a rebirth and reorganization of priorities, holds sway. As one skeptic cryptically observed to a colleague exulting over how indispensable he was to an organization: "You want to know how much you'd be missed if you dropped dead today? Put your hand into a bucket of water, then pull it out. The hole you leave is the size of the impression your absence would make!"

The reality of the transitory nature of hopes, possessions, and accomplishments is all too well-known. It has been supported by philosophers, theologians, poets, and the lives of the heroes of the pop culture. And it is obvious in man's cynicism and flight into escapism.

Of all the stresses we face in the course of our work, perhaps the greatest is the stress of wondering whether what we are doing is really worthwhile; whether our contributions make a difference. A few fortunate individuals have been blessed by God in that they can see great worth in the work they do. But for many others, the ultimate worth of what they do is an elusive mystery. Their jobs do not provide meaning. They experience periods of being painfully aware of the inevitability of their death, and of the fact that their contributions to the world seem of little consequence.

Once again, the problem is the search for meaning, for some God-sanctified purpose in life that goes beyond, as Jesus described it, just "scratching for daily bread" (Luke 12:30).

Happily, though, the stress of finding meaning—of pursuing the right purpose in life—is one that Christians *can* avoid. This can be accomplished by discovering what the Scriptures say about the various purposes that mankind has pursued throughout the ages, and discovering what the Scriptures say about the purpose God has chosen for each of us. The next two chapters will deal with better understanding how to do this.

Four
Missing the Bull's-Eye:
Is Your Life on Target?

Defeating Stress by Pursuing God's Purpose for You
Overwhelming distress and a sense of complete
purposelessness threatened to smother the spirit of
John Milton. What had been a limiting visual problem
in his early twenties had, in his mid-life, become total
blindness. The man who was destined to be hailed as
one of England's greatest poets throughout the three
centuries which followed his death wrestled agonizingly
with a cruel paradox: He knew that he had been
blessed with a talent to write—he had honed this talent
to the point that his treatises on civil and religious
issues were able to pierce to the heart of a matter like a
fine rapier—but now he was locked in darkness.

Milton struggled with the seeming hopelessness of
his blindness, pursuing an answer to the bitter
incongruity of having a unique talent that he was
unable to use to full effectiveness. Finally, the labor of
introspective searching gave birth to the sonnet, "On
His Blindness." Capitalizing on a prophetic inner
vision that penetrated the darkness with much deeper
perception than his physical eyes could ever
accomplish, Milton created an observation on the
purpose of life which was beautiful in its succinctness:

"When I consider how my light is spent,
Ere half my days in this dark world and wide,
And that one talent which is death to hide
Lodged with me useless, though my soul more bent
To serve therewith my Maker, and present
my true account, lest he returning chide,
'Doth God exact day-labor, light denied?'
I fondly ask. But Patience, to prevent
That murmur, soon replies, 'God doth not need
Either man's work or his own gifts; who best
Bear his mild yoke, they serve him best. His state
Is kingly: thousands at his bidding speed,
And post o'er land and ocean without rest;
They also serve who only stand and wait.'"

It is not, then, only those who are in the midst of the action who serve; all who are willing to bear what God has assigned to them, serve. "They also serve who only stand and wait."

Although there are those who, almost like warriors in the front lines of battle, undergo the heat of the fray and experience the brunt of the conflict, those who support them are equally important. Reserves are indispensable to the strength of an army. Without them, an army would be unable to initiate the bold maneuvers necessary to vanquish its adversary. It is not, then, only those in the midst of the action—those who unfurl the banner, carry the standard, or aggressively pursue the objective—who serve. "They also serve who only stand and wait," if that is what God has assigned them to.

King David realized this truth when he commanded his men who had been in the victorious front lines to share their plunder with the exhausted troops who, because they were too tired to fight, had remained behind with the supplies (see 1 Samuel 30:24). God gives meaning to our lives whether we are actively engaged on the front lines or quietly offering our patient willingness to be used.

The blind eyes of John Milton could see that "God's ways are not man's ways," and that there is a significance of purpose to whatever we do for God, even if that is just standing and waiting for God's clear direction. Most of us, however, make the critical mistake of using the world's temporal yardstick to measure the significance of what we do, even in measuring the worth of our *spiritual* contributions! We use this unreliable standard to decide whether we are worthy or talented enough to do certain types of God's work.

Consider the true story about a young man who, early on, sensed that his life of privilege was empty. He felt that a more significant purpose had to be served. You may be acquainted with his life:

- He was raised in the most affluent home in the nation.
- He was educated by the finest teachers of his day and studied astronomy, astrology, chemistry, physiology, mathematics, architecture, literature, and languages.
- He received a solid foundation in religious instruction at his mother's knee. (She knew he would need deeply rooted spiritual training to survive the challenges and appeal of exotic mysticism and the arrogance of privileged affluence.)
- The best of medical care and physical training were available to him. In hand-to-hand combat, against an adversary who was trained in the use of force, he was able to prevail. His keenness of eye and strength of body were such that they did not diminish with age; in his middle and later years, history tells us, he was as strong as a young man.
- He had an acute sensitivity to injustice; he was

involved in the plight of the underprivileged class.
• He had been taught that he was "someone special,"
  that the details of his birth had been God-ordained.

It was totally reasonable, logical, and defensible for
this young man to assume that his life's purpose was to
be a significant one. After all, he was educated, he had
status, he was motivated to correct injustice, he was
young and strong, and he was special. Furthermore,
everything seemed to indicate that the time was right.
Have you figured out his identity yet? Let's get more
specific:

*"One day, many years later when Moses had grown up and
become a man, he went out to visit his fellow Hebrews and
saw the terrible conditions they were under. During his
visit, he saw an Egyptian knock a Hebrew to the ground—
one of his own Hebrew brothers! Moses looked this way
and that to be sure no one was watching, then killed the
Egyptian and hid his body in the sand.*

*"The next day as he was out visiting among the
Hebrews again, he saw two of them fighting. 'What are
you doing, hitting your own Hebrew brother like that?' he
said to the one in the wrong.*

*"'And who are you?' the man demanded. 'I suppose you
think you are our prince and judge! And do you plan to
kill me as you did that Egyptian yesterday?' When Moses
realized that his deed was known, he was frightened"*
(Exodus 2:11-14).

The rest of this story is familiar. Moses fled and
ended up spending years in the pursuit of very
mundane tasks in a foreign land. One day, while
herding his sheep near the desert (and probably still
wondering about his purpose in life), Moses
encountered God, who called him to serve. But instead
of giving Moses a role that would use his self-assessed

assets of education, status, money, and connections as a mediator and authority figure for the Hebrews, God commanded Moses to be openly defiant of the powerful and arrogant Pharaoh. And for this role, this dust-caked, sweat-stained fugitive from Egyptian justice, whose temerity of youth had been replaced by the judiciousness of years spent struggling to make a living in the hot and arid land of Midian, was, in his own mind, totally unsuited for the job. In the past, yes, he might have been able to use his assets and position to ease the burdens of his brothers, but now neither the time nor the task was right. God must have made a mistake!

Using man's standard of measurement, Moses began to rationalize and argue with God (see Exodus 3:11, 13 and 4:1-18).

"I'm just not the man for the job!"
"I don't know the answers to the questions I'll be asked."
"You have no idea how skeptical people can be."
"I will lack credibility in this capacity!"
"Sure, I might have some talent, but I can't communicate well."
"You really don't know me that well, God. There has to be somebody more qualified out there. I don't want the job!"
"I'll go get some advice. Maybe I'll get a strong indication of a different direction."

The story of Moses illustrates the basic truth of Milton's poem. God has a sense of timing and purpose for each of us. This is, perhaps, the most difficult fact for us to accept, particularly if we are eager to serve him. Yet it is something we must learn, for without it we will strive for purpose (1) through the wrong endeavors, (2) at the wrong time, (3) in the wrong place.

Even Jesus, who had the most brilliantly focused,

clear-cut and unwavering vision of his life's purpose, waited thirty years before beginning his public ministry. And while he waited, he worked—at carpentry. While Moses waited, he worked at sheepherding. Joseph was a steward, Ezra was a winebearer, David was a shepherd (even *after* being anointed to be king), Peter was a fisherman, Matthew was a tax collector.

"They also," in John Milton's words, "served who only stood and waited." Each of these men, at the most beneficial time for *God's* plan, was called. And God has a unique sense of timing for each of us as well.

But one other equally important factor affects our life's purpose.

God's Unique Standard of Measurement

Often, we encounter a great deal of stress because we feel, like Moses, that though we are qualified for a significant task, God doesn't use us. We try to make ourselves available, but the harder we try the less we succeed. We become frustrated. We forget that we are serving by waiting, and we suffer great distress when we forget that God uses a different standard of measurement than we do.

When we look to the Scriptures, we find example after example of how different God's standard of measurement or evaluation really is:

- He used a boy to slay a giant (1 Samuel 17:38-50).
- He strengthened an army by commanding its leader, Gideon, to reduce its size (Judges 7:2-7).
- He used the foster daughter of a member of a minority group in a strange nation to save his people (the book of Esther).
- He used a virulent anti-Christian as his leading evangelist (Acts 9:1-19).
- He used a stable for the birthplace of the King of Kings (Luke 2:6, 7).

God places tremendous significance and value on service. All service is important. This is best summed up in Christ's statement in Mark 9:41: "If anyone so much as gives you a cup of water because you are Christ's—I say this solemnly—he won't lose his reward."

God's standard of measurement couldn't be clearer: It is Christ-honoring service to others that is the ultimate criterion of meaningfulness and purposefulness. The giving of a cup of water seems insignificant in the eyes of man—it takes little or no effort, costs no money, involves no risk, is performed without great moral or spiritual strength, and can be done as often as one would wish. But it is a significant act in the eyes of God because it is performed in the name of Jesus Christ.

So it would seem that the stress of finding meaning in our lives will be reduced in direct proportion to the extent of our response to the Holy Spirit's leading to serve others. But is this an accurate conclusion? Does the Word of God clearly support the idea that living in service to Christ will help you find meaning or purpose? This is what God says:

"If you cling to your life, you will lose it; but if you give it up for me, you will save it" (Matthew 10:39).

"For anyone who keeps his life for himself shall lose it and anyone who loses his life for me shall find it again" (Matthew 16:25).

"Anyone wanting to be the greatest must be the least— the servant of all" (Mark 9:35).

The conclusion is inescapable: We do not have to suffer distress about the significance of our purpose in life, or about finding some meaning in our lives, because God has already provided us with our purpose. The apostle Paul states this beautifully in his letter to the Christians in Ephesus: "It is God himself who has made us what we are and given us new lives from Christ Jesus, and long ages ago he planned that we should spend these lives in helping others" (Ephesians 2:10).

How Do I Start on My Life's Purpose? Now that we know we can find meaning in our lives by humbly serving others, it seems only logical that God has a task in mind for us. And it must be a task more significant than what we are doing now. After all, we know our purpose now, so we're ready for a big assignment, right? Unfortunately, this way of thinking results in the following types of situations:

The pastor who is so wrapped up in serving his congregation and in doing his duty that he neglects his own family.

The mother who organizes fund-raising activities, visits the sick, attends Bible studies, and is always ready to render service to others, but whose own children are unsupervised, unwashed, unfed, and undisciplined.

The professional person who becomes dissatisfied with his job because it is secular, and tries to make it meaningful by overtly—and obnoxiously—collaring everyone in sight and preaching at them. The result is that he not only drives everyone away, but he fails to see countless opportunities for quiet service and a Christ-like attitude right in his own department.

The person who quits his job because it's routine, or boring, or mundane, and expends his energies generating distress in trying to find "the job God really wants me to have."

We can all provide examples of well-intentioned but poorly informed Christians who have been blind to the opportunities for service that face them every day. We forget God's unique timing and his unique standard of measurement. We want to abandon our daily routines and immediately go out and slay a mighty giant on a battlefield. We forget that David had to prepare for his battle with Goliath through his daily obedience to God and his faithfulness in his job as a shepherd. We must learn to sacrifice our pride and work to maintain peace on the job or harmony in our families. Too often, good intentions result in conflicts, which result in negative stress.

But just how do we serve others, and where do we serve them? Consider the situations of each of the following people. They all wanted to serve, but felt there were no opportunities.

Mark works at the same place all day, running a lathe. The din in the plant makes conversation impossible.

Three-fifths of Dan's day is spent taking purchase or service orders on the telephone. The rest of the time is spent working alone, picking stock in the warehouse in an industrial park in Indianapolis.

Marie's work is always the same. It takes place at a long workbench and requires careful attention to detail. Though many others are nearby, it is solitary work, as cold and inhospitable as the snow-covered North Dakota plains that stretch beyond the opaque windows.

Glen's job requires making judgments. Sometimes the judgments are just hunches, guesses, or instinct. His is the kind of intuition born of three decades in the oil business. His organization depends on good judgment. Although Glen is surrounded by thousands of people in adjacent skyscrapers and on the streets of downtown Denver, there is little opportunity for "service." Independent analysis is the name of the game. Concentration on the job is the key.

Carol rarely gets to leave home. Professional and social contacts are limited. There is no obvious service to perform for anyone, other than minor household chores for family members. (In some instances, people like Carol live alone, and there are no chores to perform for anyone. There is, literally, nothing to do.)

These situations seem grim. It doesn't seem that any of these people have the place or opportunity to serve, though their desire is strong. Let's look again at what the Scriptures say about service:

"Usually a person should keep on with the work he was doing when God called him. Are you a slave? Don't let that worry you—but of course, if you get a chance to be free, take it. . . . So, dear brothers, whatever situation a person is in when he becomes a Christian, let him stay there, for now the Lord is there to help him" (1 Corinthians 7:20, 21, 24).

"Happiness or sadness or wealth should not keep anyone from doing God's work. Those in frequent contact with the exciting things the world offers should make good use of their opportunities without stopping to enjoy them; for the world in its present form will soon be gone" (1 Corinthians 7:30, 31).

"[You slaves] . . . Work hard and cheerfully at all you do, just as though you were working for the Lord and not merely for your masters . . . [The Lord] is the one you are really working for" (Colossians 3:23, 24).

"This should be your ambition: to live a quiet life, minding your own business and doing your own work, just as we told you before. As a result, people who are not Christians will trust and respect you, and you will not need to depend on others for enough money to pay your bills" (1 Thessalonians 4:11, 12).

"Kindness should begin at home . . ." (1 Timothy 5:4).

"Remind your people . . . always to be obedient and ready for any honest work" (Titus 3:1).

These Scriptures show us that our service begins wherever we are—physically, geographically, emotionally, or materially—right now. If we don't have the chance to serve others directly, then we serve them indirectly by doing the best job we can in our present circumstances. We serve God through diligent and earnest effort.

In Mark 13:9, Jesus tells the disciples to use even adversity as an opportunity to tell the Good News. In Philippians 1:12, Paul declares that everything that has happened to him in prison has been used to advance the Gospel of Jesus Christ. So we do not need to incur stress by searching for a starting point. *We are, at this moment, at the starting point. And God will take us from there.*

Understanding How to Serve. Because Satan has been so successful in appealing to our pride, the "how" of service is overlooked just as often as the "where" of service. This is why, when we are called upon to continue in what we consider a boring or mundane task, we feel disappointed. Cheated, even. Here we are, ready to charge into a battle, and all we get to do is hold up somebody else's arms while he or she dominates the scene. It doesn't matter that God placed us in the "arm-holder-upper" group instead of the high-ability "dominator" group; we want more. We forget that without someone to hold up Moses' arms, the kingdom of Israel would have been lost. (See Exodus 17:8-13.) Moses got the credit; who even remembers who held his arms up? But there are many supporters, and only a few "dominators." And most opportunities for service are not up front, dominating opportunities.

So, in the absence of exciting, stimulating, "center-stage" events, a tremendous amount of negative stress of distress is generated. And even following all the popular stress management techniques—biofeedback, exercise, diet, or whatever—doesn't help. We are frustrated and feel useless. But again, the Scriptures provide perfect instructions to manage this situation.

Scriptural Instructions on How to Serve. Let's begin with people like the shut-in, the lathe operator, and the solitary warehouse worker. How could they serve? In 1 Timothy 2:1, Paul gives the following instructions:

"Here are my directions: Pray much for others; plead for God's mercy upon them; give thanks for all he is going to do for them. Pray in this way for kings and all others who are in authority over us, or are in places of high responsibility, so that we can live in peace and quietness, spending our time in godly living and thinking much about the Lord."

Let's look for a moment at the true story of Mike Scott. Few of us have it quite as bad as Mike Scott. At age thirty, Mike had it made. He was a happy husband and father who vigorously relished the challenges of his job as a state trooper, patrolling the seemingly endless expanses of northern New Mexico's state highway system. The vagaries of the rapidly moving weather systems over the Rocky Mountains completely negated the possibility of the stress of predictability and boredom on the job. Mike loved the adventure and unpredictability of what he did!

This love extended into his off-duty pursuits, when he enjoyed drifting silently through mountain meadows and vast groves of aspen in pursuit of big game. And he was as good a hunter as he was a state trooper. The many thrills of successful hunting and fishing were crowned by the trophy buck he took one cold, gray, November morning in the late seventies. It was almost good enough to make the record books! It was what was called a "Boone and Crockett" rack; rarer than a hole-in-one in golf, a grand slam in the World Series, or a hat trick in the Stanley Cup playoffs! He would have the head mounted; a trophy to grace his den and to serve as the focal point of a story to regale his visitors with in years to come.

The head now overpoweringly dominates Mike's room at the nursing home. It looks totally incongruous in an environment populated almost completely by the aged and the mentally and physically infirm. It looms, almost, over Mike's bed, where the once-robust, two-hundred-and-twenty-pound trooper lies motionless, completely paralyzed, a frail, eighty-five-pound victim of a completely unexpected stroke. It leveled him with terrifying suddenness one evening in 1979, when he was thirty, as he started to walk across his den for a snack while watching TV.

From that horrifying instant when he found himself crumpled on the floor, unable to move a muscle or utter a sound, Mike has endured the agony of confinement in a motionless body. His mind still wanders the mountains of New Mexico, still thrashes to communicate his joys and sorrows to his loved ones, and screams to express his torture to his brothers and sisters in Christ. But how does anyone know Mike's mind is active? He can roll his eyes upward to communicate when a letter is pointed at on a huge alphabet board that hangs on the wall, adjacent to his lifelike, but lifeless, buck head mount.

Mike Scott's life seems totally devoid of ever having a significant purpose—even by God's standard of measurement. It doesn't appear that he can possibly make a contribution to anyone. But Mike, whose mind is as healthy and active as it ever was, *can* serve through praying for "God's mercy on others . . . for kings, and for all others who are in authority over us, or in places of high responsibility." He can perform a task regarded as so significant by Jesus that he went into the mountains and "prayed all night." Prayer is so significant that it changed the course of history when Elijah prayed for no rain, and a three-year drought ensued. When he prayed again, this time for an end to the drought, the rains were spilled from the heavens.

Mike Scott *can* serve, and he is unwaveringly aware of his purpose. In fact, the first sentence he spelled out brought a young Christian man to his knees. Darold, a total stranger, came to visit Mike, hoping to minister to him. As he awkwardly pointed to individual letters on Mike's alphabet board, Mike laboriously rolled his eyes upward in response and spelled out "I l-o-v-e J-e-s-u-s." Darold found that *he* was the one ministered to through Mike's constant faith and service.

Other Ways to Serve: What God Says: It's obvious from Scripture that we can serve others through praying for them. But the Bible is equally explicit in laying out other ways we can serve. Each of the following Scriptures gives examples of service that are possible for anyone who comes into contact with other people, even if direct verbal communication does not take place:

"If your gift is that of serving others, serve them well. If you are a teacher, do a good job of teaching. If you are a preacher, see to it that your sermons are strong and helpful. If God has given you money, be generous in helping others with it . . . Don't just pretend that you love others: really love them. Hate what is wrong. Stand on the side of the good. Love each other with brotherly affection and take delight in honoring each other. Never be lazy in your work but serve the Lord enthusiastically.

"Be glad for all God is planning for you. Be patient in trouble, and prayerful always. When God's children are in need, you be the one to help them out. And get into the habit of inviting guests home for dinner or, if they need lodging, for the night.

"If someone mistreats you because you are a Christian, don't curse him; pray that God will bless him. When others

are happy, be happy with them. If they are sad, share their sorrow. Work happily together. Don't try to act big. Don't try to get into the good graces of important people, but enjoy the company of ordinary folks. And don't think you know it all!

"Never pay back evil for evil. Do things in such a way that everyone can see you are honest clear through. Don't quarrel with anyone. Be at peace with everyone, just as much as possible.

"Dear friends, never avenge yourselves. Leave that to God, for he has said that he will repay those who deserve it. [Don't take the law into your own hands.] Instead, feed your enemy if he is hungry. If he is thirsty give him something to drink and you will be 'heaping coals of fire on his head.' In other words, he will feel ashamed of himself for what he has done to you. Don't let evil get the upper hand but conquer evil by doing good" (Romans 12:7-21).

"We must bear the 'burden' of being considerate of the doubts and fears of others—of those who feel these things are wrong. Let's please the other fellow, not ourselves, and do what is for his good and thus build him up in the Lord" (Romans 15:2).

"In fact, in everything we do we try to show that we are true ministers of God. We patiently endure suffering and hardship and trouble of every kind. . . . We stand true to the Lord whether others honor us or despise us, whether they criticize us or commend us . . ." (2 Corinthians 6:4, 8).

"Share each other's troubles and problems, and so obey our Lord's command. If anyone thinks he is too great to stoop to do this, he is fooling himself. He is really a nobody. Let everyone be sure that he is doing his very best, for then he will have the personal satisfaction of work well done, and won't need to compare himself with someone else. . . . Whenever we can we should always be kind to everyone, and especially to our Christian brothers" (Galatians 6:2-4, 10).

"Slaves, obey your masters; be eager to give them your

very best. Serve them as you would Christ. Don't work hard only when your master is watching and then shirk when he isn't looking; work hard and with gladness all the time, as though working for Christ, doing the will of God with all your hearts" (Ephesians 6:5-7).

"Never let it be said that Christ's people are poor workers. Don't let the name of God or his teaching be laughed at because of this" (1 Timothy 6:1).

"You yourself must be an example . . . of good deeds of every kind. Let everything you do reflect your love of the truth and the fact that you are in dead earnest about it" (Titus 2:7).

"It is God's will that your good lives should silence those who foolishly condemn the Gospel without knowing what it can do for them, having never experienced its power. . . . Show respect for everyone. Love Christians everywhere. Fear God and honor the government" (1 Peter 2:15, 17).

Service is an attitude. It is giving diligent attention to your work, and being sensitive to the needs of others. Although we can list possible overt actions based on the Scriptures listed above, our service must go beyond "being kind." Our service is, in short, to live in love.

"Unimportant" Situations: Why They're Important. In a bland mixture, salt is *never* without effect. In a dark room, even a flicker of light makes an impact. The moment your attitude of service begins, your stress starts to diminish. And your attitude of service can begin in even the briefest relationships or encounters, especially when you realize that—for the Christian— there are no unimportant people, situations, or relationships.

You see, you are a part of the environment of every other person you meet. So even encounters as brief as a few moments—a shared elevator trip or a purchase in a store—are significant. We inevitably affect the environment of others with whom we come into contact, thereby adding to, detracting from, or neutralizing their effectiveness by our actions. When we realize this, it becomes evident that how well or how positively we respond to others becomes very important.

Any situation in which we find ourselves should be improved because we are Christians and we are there. And the more situations improve, the more likely it is that those people involved will become relaxed and open to the positive influence of Christ through us. So, in this sense, everything we do is important. As Paul says in 1 Corinthians 10:31, "Whatsoever you do, do all to the glory of God."

Six Steps to Managing the Stress of Purposelessness

The following six-step plan for managing the stress of purposelessness can be successful in any situation, at any time, in any place. It is the embodiment of the promise of 1 John 1:4, "If you do as I say . . . then you, too, will be full of joy, and so will we."

Jesus also stated this promise in the Gospel of John. He had demonstrated true service by washing the feet of his disciples, and then he said, "I have given you an example to follow: do as I have done to you . . . You know these things—now do them! That is the path of blessing" (John 13:15, 17).

The plan is as follows:

Step One: Evaluate the seven basic purposes or goals pursued by mankind throughout the ages. Discover what Scripture says the pursuit of each of these goals leads to. (See Chapter 5.)

Step Two: Write down the purpose or goal pursued by the evangelists, by the apostles, and by Jesus. Discover what the Scripture says the pursuit of this goal leads to. (See page 51.)

Step Three: Consider the fact that God will place a willing servant where he or she is best used. Realize that God has a unique sense of timing in the lives of believers, and a unique sense of measurement for the value of their service. (See page 48.)

Step Four: Ask the Holy Spirit for understanding of Jesus's words in Matthew 10:39 and Luke 9:24.

Step Five: Regard your present situation as the starting point for service. Make a list of the opportunities God has provided—however trivial they may appear—in both social and occupational settings, always keeping Step Three in mind. Develop your list by using the work page at the end of this chapter.

Step Six: Act upon your opportunities for service. The stress of purpose*less*ness cannot coexist with the joy of purpose*ful*ness. Jesus said, "My purpose is to give life in all its fullness" (John 10:10). A full life is one with a purpose. For the Christian, a purposeful life is one of service. So, to find your purpose, find your service.

Summary
Even the most brilliantly devised and carefully crafted secular formulas for stress management cannot effectively cope with the stress of trying to find a purpose in life. And such stress will only increase when we measure our achievements by man's standards, and fail to achieve "greater things." But this stress can be managed to the point that it is virtually nonexistent, by understanding God's unique sense of timing and standards of measurements for each of us, his children. It is God who magnifies our lowest service, so that there are no "greater things" to pursue. The "how" of our service to God lies in our attitude. The "where" of this service is wherever we are right now.

Opportunities for Service
This page is to be used in Step Five in the Six-Step Plan for managing the stress of finding a purpose in your life.

Read the Scripture in the column on the left, then list the nature of the service that it reflects.

Scripture Reference	Service Possible Now
1 Corinthians 16:5, 6	
2 Corinthians 5:15	
2 Corinthians 6:3, 4	
Ephesians 1:12	
Ephesians 2:10	
Philippians 4:5	
Colossians 3:18, 19	
Colossians 3:23, 24	
1 Thessalonians 4:11, 12	
2 Timothy 1:3	
Titus 3:14	
Hebrews 6:10	
Hebrews 10:24	
Hebrews 13:16	
James 1:9	
1 Peter 5:2	
1 John 3:17, 18	
1 John 4:7, 8	

Five
Your Unlucky Number: Why You Pick It

"I've Got Your Number!"

What does it mean when somebody "has your number"? Simply this—that he knows your point of vulnerability. He knows what you're up to, and what motivates you. Yet, while we can determine somebody else's motivation, we often are ignorant about our own. Generally, we haven't taken the time to think about it, or we don't know how to analyze ourselves. But understanding what motivates us is a vital step to successful stress management! Unless motivation is understood, goals and plans are haphazard at best.

If the activities of unbelievers (and, unfortunately, many believers as well) are analyzed, they can generally be placed into one of seven basic goal categories:

1. *Physical Pleasure.* Hedonism: The titillation or excitement of the senses (touch, taste, smell, hearing, and seeing).
2. *Honors and Popularity.* Formal and informal admiration received for one's accomplishments, possessions, or personal qualities such as physical appearance or intelligence.
3. *Prestige and Social Status.* Power through acknowledgment by others of one's professional or social relationships, achievements, or status.

4. *Wealth.* The accumulating of valued commodities, including precious metals, currency, art, real estate, and other culturally-accepted symbols of wealth.

5. *Achievement.* The creating of enduring monuments in art, music, literature, or architecture, or by the establishing of one's "place" in history.

6. *Security.* The constructing of personal, social, and financial barriers to adversity for one's loved ones and oneself.

7. *Personal Purity.* Self-righteousness or personal piety; works-oriented virtue in the pursuit of "rightness" with God. Altruism, or the pursuit of "service" to mankind through the giving of time, talent, or possessions.

The unspiritual man is drawn irresistibly to at least one of these seven goals; his basic nature makes it impossible for him not to pursue them. The apostle Paul realized this, and warned the Christians in Rome to seek a new outlook to life: "Don't copy the behavior and customs of this world, but be a new and different person with a fresh newness in all you do and think" (Romans 12:2).

The non-Christians of Paul's day (like many of our day) were dedicated to achieving one or more of the seven goals. The Spirit-led person, however, knows innately that the pursuit of any of these basic goals will ultimately lead to stress and emptiness. He knows this because he possesses insight which the unspiritual person does not. "But the spiritual man has insight into everything, and that bothers and baffles the man of the world, who can't understand him at all" (1 Corinthians 2:15).

And he can grow in this insight through studying

and applying the Word of God: "And be sure to put into practice what you hear. The more you do this, the more you will understand what I tell you" (Mark 4:24). This insight into the folly of being goal-driven rather than God-led is best expressed by a man who, at one point, achieved every one of the seven goals listed above! Nevertheless, he prayed: "Lord, help me to realize how brief my time on earth will be. Help me to know that I am here for but a moment more. My life is no longer than my hand! My whole lifetime is but a moment to you. Proud man! Frail as breath! A shadow! And all his busy rushing ends in nothing. He heaps up riches for someone else to spend" (Psalm 39:4-6). His name? David, king of Israel.

David's wisdom came from being God-led. He knew how short life was and how futile human strivings are. And this knowledge was painful to bear. "For the more my wisdom, the more my grief; to increase knowledge only increases distress," lamented Solomon, the second-wisest man who ever lived, in Ecclesiastes 1:18. God inspired these men to share their awareness of the futility of pursuing anything but God-ordained goals. As we grow in wisdom and become more and more "other-world" oriented, we, too, will suffer grief over our brothers and sisters who strive for perishable goals, who, in the process, suffer self-created distress.

But how, exactly, does the pursuit of inappropriate goals create stress? (And remember, we are not talking here about *managing unavoidable* stress, but about *avoiding unmanageable* stress.)

Let's begin with Goal #1, and do a goal-by-goal evaluation of what God says about each one.

Goal #1: *Personal Pleasure—Living for a Good Time.* If we follow our own inclinations to live for pleasure, and if we are not Spirit-led, God tells us what will happen:

"But when you follow your own wrong inclinations your lives will produce these evil results: impure thoughts, eagerness for lustful pleasure, idolatry, spiritism (that is, encouraging the activity of demons), hatred and fighting, jealousy and anger, constant effort to get the best for yourself, complaints and criticisms, the feeling that everyone else is wrong except those in your own little group—and there will be wrong doctrine, envy, murder, drunkenness, wild parties, and all that sort of thing. Let me tell you again as I have before, that anyone living that sort of life will not inherit the kingdom of God" (Galatians 5:19-21).

"Their future is eternal loss, for their god is their appetite: they are proud of what they should be ashamed of; and all they think about is this life here on earth" (Philippians 3:19).

"Away then with sinful, earthly things; deaden the evil desires lurking within you; have nothing to do with sexual sin, impurity, lust and shameful desires; don't worship the good things of life, for that is idolatry. God's terrible anger is upon those who do such things" (Colossians 3:5, 6).

God is very clear about the results of living only for pleasure. This gives us an incisive insight into stress management from a Christian perspective: The pursuit of "self-fulfillment" or pleasure will always lead to stress. Let's translate this into modern terms. A life of partying, loafing, traveling, and pursuing the "good things of life" creates a self-centered existence. While it might not become as extreme as the one described in Galatians by Paul, it is, in essence, the same type of life-style. Therefore, it will lead to the same stresses of hatred, fighting, quarreling, backbiting, complaining, paranoia, envy, overindulgence in food and drink, and so on.

Now, turn the coin over. God tells us in the very next verses of that Scripture what we will experience if we are guided by the Holy Spirit: "But when the Holy Spirit controls our lives he will produce this kind of fruit in us: love, joy, peace, patience, kindness, goodness, faithfulness, gentleness, and self-control" (Galatians 5:22).

Goal #2: *Honors and Popularity.* How important is it to be honored and popular? According to the August 1983 issue of *Muscle and Fitness,* it is important enough to young athletes that, in a survey of aspiring Olympians, over half of them stated that they would be willing to take a pill which would kill them within a year if taking it would guarantee that they could first win a gold medal!

It is the cornerstone of the basic mores of inter-personal relations in many cultures in the Far East. The concept of "face" ("keeping face," "saving face," and not threatening another's "face") requires intricate attention to a whole array of nuances of social behavior.

This goal was strong enough to cause dissension among the disciples, and it was the motivation for the preaching of the Gospel by self-appointed evangelists eager to embarrass and humiliate the apostle Paul. (See Mark 9:34 and Philippians 1:15.)

This desire for recognition has caused otherwise sensible men and women of all ages and walks of life to engage in behaviors that have resulted in the loss of their possessions, families, self-respect, health, and, tragically, even their lives.

Several negative behaviors and emotions accompany the pursuit of honors and popularity: We compare ourselves with others, and if we don't compare favorably we become frustrated or get caught up in self-delusive rationalization. We rarely relax socially, because we always feel "on stage." Often we adopt ill-fitting behaviors which are merely a "front." We give in and go along with the prevailing values of the peer group, which generally leaves us with a guilty conscience. We try to deal with our frustration and bitterness, yet still fail to achieve our social or professional goals. We end up adapting our recreation and schedules to the preferences of others. Finally, we participate in slander or gossip, pushing others down in order to push ourselves up.

Each of these behaviors causes stress, and each one is a natural by-product of the pursuit of honors and popularity. But the spiritual person can learn how to avoid these by immersing himself in the Word of God:

"We won't need to look for honors and popularity, which lead to jealousy and hard feelings" (Galatians 5:26).

"Let everyone be sure that he is doing his very best, for then he will have the personal satisfaction of work well done, and won't need to compare himself with someone else" (Galatians 6:4).

"Don't be selfish; don't live to make a good impression on others. Be humble, thinking of others as better than yourself" (Philippians 2:3).

"Since you have been chosen by God who has given you this new kind of life, and because of his deep love and concern for you, you should practice tenderhearted mercy and kindness to others. Don't worry about making a good impression on them but be ready to suffer quietly and patiently" (Colossians 3:12).

"For jealousy and selfishness are not God's kind of wisdom. Such things are earthly, unspiritual, inspired by the devil. For wherever there is jealousy or selfish ambition, there will be disorder and every other kind of evil" (James 3:15, 16).

Goal #3: *Prestige and Social Status.* "The Unsinkable Molly Brown" is the story of the indomitable wife of a mining tycoon who struck it rich in the ore-laden mines of Leadville, Colorado. Molly, who, as a baby, survived the sinking of the Titanic, demonstrates the distinction between honors and popularity (Goal #2) and prestige and social status (Goal #3). Molly enjoyed honors, fame, and popularity, but she could never break into the zealously guarded ranks of Denver's elite high society. She did everything possible to be accepted. She hungered for the power, prestige, and esteem of the "in" group.

Yet, the goals of honors and popularity, and prestige and social status, are intertwined. They are woven together by the common strand of pride. This third goal leads to yet another assortment of stress-inducing behaviors.

"Workaholism" becomes a tool to attain a higher position, more power, and more perceived status. Overspending and conspicuous consumption are used to create the illusion of wealth and power.

Financial overcommitment results from speculative ventures in the hope of one "big break." Even worse is personal overcommitment, often at the expense of family, to "status" tasks in the local or larger community, or even in the church! And many fall into personally or spiritually destructive behavior, when they know better. (Herod's beheading of John in Matthew 14:1-12 is a tragic example of prestige-driven behavior.)

God's Word again becomes the source for understanding the stresses of this negative goal:

"Woe to you Pharisees! For how you love the seats of honor in the synagogues and the respectful greetings from everyone as you walk through the markets! Yes, awesome judgment is awaiting you" (Luke 18:14).

"For the proud shall be humbled, but the humble shall be honored" (Luke 18:14).

"What is causing the quarrels and fights among you? Isn't it because there is a whole army of evil desires within you?" (James 4:1).

The most agonizing burden of prestige-driven stress ever recorded is the account of the attitude of the Jewish leaders recorded in John 12:42, 43: "However, even many of the Jewish leaders believed him to be the Messiah but wouldn't admit it to anyone because of their fear that the Pharisees would excommunicate them from the synagogue; for they loved the praise of men more than the praise of God."

Imagine the incredible spiritual turmoil the Jewish leaders experienced, knowing full well that they had chosen temporary status over eternal salvation!

Stress-avoiding behaviors are possible through the development of God-directed attitudes toward prestige and social status. Jesus provides us with a perfect example of this God-directed attitude in John 5:41, in response to the current power structure's rejection of him:

"Your approval or disapproval means nothing to me," [he declared in response to the Jewish leaders who had rejected him], "for as I know so well, you don't have God's love within you."

Jesus' words provide an illuminating insight into the fact that we often incur stress because, incredibly, we strive for approval: (1) from those who reject our Savior; or (2) on the basis of criteria which are not Christ-honoring.

Do you want to totally avoid the stress of not being accepted by the power elite, the "in" group, or the boss? Use Jesus' criterion: *Approval or disapproval by others counts only to the extent that God's purposes are honored.* There is no other criterion.

This criterion is stated again in Colossians 3:11: "In this new life one's nationality or race or education or social position is unimportant; such things mean nothing. Whether a person has Christ is what matters, and he is equally available to all."

In essence, Paul is saying, "Don't worry about making a good impression on [others]" (v. 12), and he elaborates upon his advice in his letter to the Romans: "As God's messenger I give each of you God's warning: Be honest in your estimate of yourselves, measuring your value by how much faith God has given you" (Romans 12:3).

It is totally unnecessary to feel stress because you aren't known or among "important" people. This stress will not become even a secondary or tertiary motivator if you can remember to concentrate instead on the only criterion that really matters—faith in God.

Goal #4: *Wealth and Material Success.* It's a well-known fact that material success is a compelling motivator. Wealth is even heralded by well-meaning preachers (and not-so-well-meaning wolves-in-sheep's-clothing) who pander to our greed to get us to make financial contributions. Thousands upon thousands of Christians are led to the surreptitious hope that giving to God will result in a monetary return rather than in blessings of another type.

In the secular arena, tales abound of hard-driving "Type A" executives who, like some adventure-motivated hero in a fairy tale, abandon home and family to "seek their fortune." Yet, they ultimately find that they have paid the bitter price of lost self-respect, empty marriages, alienated offspring, and, in many cases, ruined health or premature death.

A fascinating insight about the pursuit and possession of material wealth is that it is the people who have "been there" who most often point out the folly of pursuing money. King David, one of the richest of men, placed material wealth in its proper perspective by sharing his insight into the fleeting nature of life:

"Lord . . . when you punish a man for his sins, he is
destroyed, for he is as fragile as a moth-infested cloth;
yes, man is frail as breath. Hear my prayer, O Lord;
listen to my cry! Don't sit back, unmindful of my tears.
For I am your guest. I am a traveler passing through the
earth, as all my fathers were. Spare me Lord! Let me
recover and be filled with happiness again before my
death" (Psalm 39:10-13).

Solomon, whose material wealth was mind-boggling,
was led by the Holy Spirit to this insight: "Don't weary
yourself trying to get rich. Why waste your time? For
riches can disappear as though they had the wings of a
bird!" (Proverbs 23:4, 5).

Not only was material wealth not worth pursuing,
but it was a goal that, if attained, brought with it grave
danger. The Book of Proverbs includes a prayer about
this: "Give me neither poverty nor riches! Give me just
enough to satisfy my needs! For if I grow rich, I may
become content without God" (Proverbs 30:8, 9).

This same danger, the danger of a false sense of
security or a focus away from spiritual things, was
pointedly emphasized by Jesus himself in such
Scriptures as Mark 10:24, 25; Luke 6:24, 25; 18:13, 14.

When we trust in riches, becoming totally enamored
of the things of this world, we risk the loss of eternal
life! Jesus' warning (in Luke 12) about squandering the
things of real value in pursuit of riches was asserted in
the form of a parable, and the lesson is so obvious that
only the willfully ignorant could miss the point.

*"Then he gave an illustration: 'A rich man had a fertile
farm that produced fine crops. In fact, his barns were full
to overflowing—he couldn't get everything in. He thought
about his problem, and finally exclaimed, "I know—I'll
tear down my barns and build bigger ones! Then I'll have
room enough. And I'll sit back and say to myself, 'Friend,
you have enough stored away for years to come. Now take*

it easy! Wine, women and song for you!'" But God said to him, "Fool! Tonight you die. Then who will get it all?" Yes, every man is a fool who gets rich on earth but not in heaven'" (Luke 12:16-21).

And in Mark 8:36, Jesus points out that even all the wealth the world is not worth the loss of eternal life: "And how does a man benefit if he gains the whole world and loses his soul in the process?"

What else does God say about having material wealth as a goal? The apostle Paul describes the detrimental results of longing for riches: "But people who long to be rich soon begin to do all kinds of wrong things to get money, things that hurt them and make them evil-minded and finally send them to hell itself. For the love of money is the first step toward all kinds of sin. Some people have even turned away from God because of their love for it, and as a result have pierced themselves with many sorrows" (1 Timothy 6:9-10).

To avoid the distresses of pursuing wealth, God provides this simple solution: "Do you want to be truly rich? You already are if you are happy and good. After all, we didn't bring any money with us when we came into the world, and we can't carry away a single penny when we die. So we should be well satisfied without money if we have enough food and clothing" (1 Timothy 6:6-8).

Suppose, though, that God has blessed you with material prosperity for your diligent effort to serve him. Again, his Word provides a method of avoiding the distress of prosperity:

"Tell those who are rich not to be proud and not to trust in their money, which will soon be gone, but their pride and trust should be in the living God who always richly gives us all we need for our enjoyment. Tell them to use their money to do good. They should be rich in good works and

should give happily to those in need, always being ready to share with others whatever God has given them. By doing this they will be storing up real treasure for themselves in heaven—it is the only safe investment for eternity! And they will be living a fruitful Christian life down here as well" (1 Timothy 6:17-19).

There is yet one additional insight about the distress which often occurs when money is involved. A wrong emphasis on money—even for people of moderately comfortable means—can also create distress. In Luke 16:13, Jesus teaches a profound truth: "For neither you nor anyone else can serve two masters. You will hate one and show loyalty to the other, or else the other way around—you will be enthusiastic about one and despise the other. You cannot serve both God and money."

The Word of God is clear: If money comes before God, distress is sure to follow. If material wealth is our goal in life, even if we succeed in reaching our goal, distress will be an unavoidable result! And if we cannot make a total commitment one way or the other—if we are "just a little" less generous than we ought to be, or "just a little" less dedicated to the support of Kingdom work than we ought to be, we have an implied guarantee from Jesus himself: We will suffer distress.

Goal #5: *Achievement—Securing One's Place in History.* Forty-first Street, Miami Beach, Florida. What does it mean to you? For most of us, it's just a number. But for one person, it was evidence of the tremendous impact he had generated on the city of Miami Beach as the most popular entertainer in the country. For in 1953, Forty-first Street was renamed "Arthur Godfrey Road." This tremendous honor was meant to be a lasting testimony to the contribution the versatile Godfrey had made in the rise to prominence of the community that was "home" to his radio and television show. The idol of millions, Godfrey beamed with pleasure at the recognition. He had made his mark.

Twenty-five years later, however, Arthur Godfrey Road was again renamed—to Forty-first Street. Just a number. "Arthur Godfrey means nothing to this community anymore," the City Commissioner observed. Once the most popular name in America, "Arthur Godfrey" now evokes a blank look from college students three decades after the official act to preserve his memory for posterity.

It was, in essence, the same fate which befell one of Arthur Godfrey's contemporaries, a man whose blustering threats were dutifully reported in every major news service in the world. This man's most mundane comments were analyzed by intelligence sources for even a minute inkling of his intentions. But with the fleeting temporariness of a shadow gliding across a sunswept plain, Nikita Khrushchev passed into oblivion. Shortly after his death, he was relegated by the government of the U.S.S.R. to the status of "nonperson" and buried, by official decision, in a simple cemetery, in a grave indistinguishable from the unadorned plots of the common people.

"Those who cannot remember the past," observed philosopher-writer George Santayana, "are condemned to repeat it." And this frequently quoted statement has validity even on a personal level. We can strive for acclaim and lasting renown, but history convincingly teaches the lesson that even the most determined achiever will ultimately be swallowed up in the enshrouding realm of disappointing obscurity.

What kind of achievement, then, is worth striving for? Despite the fact that he sought to deeply imbue his disciples with an "other-world" orientation, it was necessary for Jesus to remind them of the transitory nature of temporary accomplishment. "All these buildings will be knocked down, with not one stone left

on top of another," he said of the temple in Matthew
24:2, when his disciples were marveling at its grandeur.
It was a lesson he taught again and again. A lesson
which, if ignored, Jesus warned, would result in the
loss of eternal life (see Matthew 16:26). For the
underlying motivation fueling man's desire to secure
his "place" in history is pride. And there is no shortage
of warning in the Scriptures against pride and its
disastrous consequences.

Pride—the desire for immortality through accomplishment—always brings distress. For the spiritual
person, distress results from his awareness of God's
admonitions against pride. And for both the unspiritual
person and the spiritual person, distress comes from an
awareness that no earthly accomplishment is
guaranteed to last.

Forty-first Street. "Just a number."

Goal #6: *Security.* There is no argument that security, the
desire to protect ourselves in any eventuality, is a major
motivational force in the world of commerce. Financial
institutions advertise it and create the illusion of it;
investment institutions promise it. Whole industries
with products ranging from smoke detectors to guard
dogs to electronic surveillance systems, are founded on
providing it.

And yet, while billions of dollars are poured into the
business of "security," there remains an undeniable
awareness by even the most careful of planners that
complete security is an illusion—pursuable, but not
attainable. The fact will always remain that *we are
vulnerable.*

Perhaps the most striking admission of our
vulnerability was the cynicism shown, in the mid-
eighties, in the demands of college students that
campus health services stockpile cyanide tablets in the
event of nuclear war. Security, the students realized,

was an illusion, a construct of fantasy. Death was the only unassailable sanctuary—an ultimate escape to the "total security" of oblivion.

The Scriptures state that the pursuit of security apart from God is vain folly. James, in the fourth chapter of his epistle, provides a chastening reminder of the tenuousness of life and of our utter dependence upon God: "Look here, you people who say 'Today or tomorrow we are going to such and such a town, stay there a year, and open up a profitable business.' How do you know what is going to happen tomorrow? For the length of your lives is as uncertain as the morning fog—now you see it; soon it is gone. What you ought to say is, 'If the Lord wants us to, we shall live and do this or that'" (James 4:13-15).

The Lord knew that insecurity was exacting its toll in a high price of anxiety and fear among the people of his time. He intimately indentified with the distress of the crowds who were threatened by the power of foreign occupation and the corruption of their civil and religious leaders. In Luke 12:4, 5, Jesus addressed their concerns: "Dear friends, don't be afraid of these who want to murder you. They can only kill the body; they have no power over your souls. But I'll tell you whom to fear—fear God who has the power to kill and then cast into hell."

And as they anxiously pondered a future fraught with threatening uncertainty, Jesus further responded to their distress: "So don't be anxious about tomorrow. God will take care of your tomorrow too. Live one day at a time" (Matthew 6:34).

Some problems require great wisdom and insight before truth can be seen and understood. But the truth for Goal #6 is obvious: Regardless of anything we do—of the intricacies of our financial, political, social, and personal networks and alliances—security will be tenuous at best. Uncertainty will always loom in the darkness, the unvanquished, ever-present witness to man's ultimate vulnerability in a hostile world.

Goal #7: *Personal Piety.* "We are all infected and impure with sin. When we put on our prized robes of righteousness we find that they are but filthy rags." In Isaiah 64:6 the prophet accurately predicts the outcome of thorough self-analysis following self-sacrifice. We are, quite obviously, inadequate. Our best, he declares, is our worst. The vestments we consider to be virtuous are only tawdry and shabby evidence of vice to God.

Unavoidable stress. It is, once again, identified as both the temporal and eternal experience of those who pursue self-righteousness or piety as a life goal. For when self-purification becomes a goal, introspective analysis will inevitably take place. And intelligent introspective analysis always produces the unanswerable question of "How much is enough?"

Christians, however, should not experience the distress of Goal #7. The testimony of the apostle Paul, who suffered this distress before he was blessed with Spirit-bestowed insight, tells why:

"But all these things that I once thought very worthwhile—now I've thrown them all away so that I can put my trust and hope in Christ alone. Yes, everything else is worthless when compared with the priceless gain of knowing Christ Jesus my Lord. I have put aside all else, counting it worth less than nothing, in order that I can have Christ, and become one with him, no longer counting on being saved by being good enough or by obeying God's laws, but by trusting Christ to save me; for God's way of making us right with himself depends on faith—counting on Christ alone" (Philippians 3:7-9).

Unlucky Numbers and Expert Witnesses
Will the pursuit of one or more of the goals in this
chapter always lead to distress? Three witnesses can be
called upon to provide testimony to the validity of this
conclusion:

1. *Logical Analysis,* which will readily expose the
   ultimate meaninglessness of each goal.
2. *History,* which provides case histories of lives
   wasted in the pursuit of illusions.
3. *The Scriptures,* which explicitly and implicitly
   describe the disastrous results of an all-
   encompassing pursuit of any of the goals
   presented in this chapter.

Is all then, as Solomon exclaimed, merely "vanity"? Is
there anything worth working for? Yes! For those who
live the abundant life in Jesus Christ, there is no
"unlucky number." There is no distress as a result of
pursuing wrong goals, for when one is submitted to the
Spirit of God, the most rewarding goal of all comes into
existence. This goal is summarized by this simple
statement:

*"Only one life, 'twill soon be past,
Only what's done for Christ will last"* (Anonymous).

Six
People Problems: The Stress of Imperfect Relationships

Real People: Real Problems

"Lord, help me to pray for others at least as often as I am tempted to criticize them."

Two keys for unlocking the secret of dealing with imperfect relationships, or "people problems," are implicit in the simple little prayer above. A vast number of interpersonal problems would disappear, or might never even emerge, if these words were diligently prayed each day. That's not to say the problems of relationships will disappear. People problems will always be present, and will always create stress.

While it is not possible to describe in detail every conceivable problem, it is possible to classify people problems into certain categories, or types. You may, in fact, recognize your particular sources of stress in one or more of the descriptions below.

Roberta is a concerned professional in a large corporation which rigidly adheres to the "lines of authority" concept. That is, if you have a problem with company policy, working conditions, job description, or any facet of your employment, you process your problem through "proper channels"—first to the department head, then to the section head, then to the division head, then to the vice president of marketing, and so forth.

Unfortunately, Roberta works for a department head who intensely dislikes her. Roberta feels this is partially because she is a competent woman who is assertive and capable, and the department head apparently has problems accepting women in leadership roles. He has made it clear to her that her performance evaluation will be such that bonuses or other perks will be impossible for her, regardless of how well she does her job. She consistently receives undesirable assignments or difficult clients, making it impossible for her to even mentally "escape" into doing a good job. In brief, she is the victim of a Machiavellian personality who is amoral, and who seems to delight in making life difficult for her.

Roberta knows what he's doing, but she can't prove it. And even if she could, the seeming pledge of total silence among the administrative hierarchy has emphatically slammed the door that could lead to equitable treatment for her. She is distressed because the corporate "channel" structure has made it impossible for her to elicit remedial action from anyone up the ladder from the department head, since it seems that administrators "cover" for one another.

Keith's situation is very similar. But there is one striking difference: Keith knows ways to combat the power play; subtle ways to make his "chameleon" supervisor turn the wrong color at the wrong time and expose himself. In essence, Keith can get even and get rid of his supervisor without ever having to tip his hand. But there's a problem—Keith is a Christian. So he chooses *not* to expose the man, even though he can. Instead, Keith puts up with the power plays by people who mistakenly interpret his nonretaliatory attitude as professional or intellectual impotence. They take advantage of him and he refuses to use the avenues he could to effectively cut them off, because those methods would not be God-pleasing. The more Christian he is, the more uncharitable they become.

And then there is Andrea. She seems to have it all—confidence, intelligence, and good looks. She conveys an "I'm okay" attitude in any situation. Often she's preoccupied, self-entertained with projects and activities at home, at church, and in her recreational pursuits. She has become unfairly labled as arrogant, stuck-up, vain, or antisocial. She's victimized by petty gossip which alludes to her supposed character deficiencies.

In reality, Andrea *is* confident—in Christ. She realizes her intelligence is not a result of achievement and that her physical attractiveness is an "accident of birth." She works at maintaining her health through exercise and diet and she minds her own business at work and does a good job. She is not unfriendly, but she's reserved—a private person. And she is torn to pieces by the vicious gossip of coworkers and jealous peers.

What's Your Imperfect Interpersonal Relationship?
The situations described previously are real problems currently being faced by real people. They are actual case histories of the three kinds of work-related relationship problems described below:

1. Personal or professional vulnerability to an individual or organization who can victimize a person with "power plays" or with deliberately vindictive decisions.
2. Personal or professional vulnerability through

being taken advantage of because one is committed to living a loving, nonretaliatory Christian life.

3. Perceiving undeserved hostility as a result of the inaccurate impressions or wrong opinions others have formed.

Other relationship problems, both work- and non-work-related include:

4. Not being allowed to express abilities, talents, or capacity to be productive because of intentional or unintentional impediments imposed by others.

5. Coping with a relationship that is unpleasant and perhaps even spiritually debilitating, but inescapable.

6. Being faced with the threat of the success of others with whom you are placed in either explicit or implicit competition.

7. Surviving rejection by someone you love.

8. Watching your rights being violated, your self-concept being deprecated, and your dignity being assaulted as a result of someone's unintentional insensitivity or his intentional malevolence.

9. Putting yourself on the line for your basic beliefs and values.

10. Meeting expectations which are unreasonable, unrealistic, or unattainable.

11. Facing the reality of your total inability to change the behavior of someone you love who is chemically dependent or otherwise spiritually incapacitated by God-dishonoring goals, desires, associations, or activities.

12. Living with the stress of romantic love for someone who is not your spouse or who is married to someone else.

Whether a problem is one with someone on a different level (employee to employer, child to parent) or one that is peer-to-peer (coworker to coworker, neighbor to neighbor, brother to sister), almost all interpersonal problems can be identified under one or more of the categories described above.

Even if a relationship is one similar to item twelve and it is impossible to anticipate the outcome, or if the Scriptures do not explicitly spell out what to do, the stress of the relationship can still be managed. It can be managed because it is not always necessary to conjecture about what you *will* do if something happens as long as you are unequivocal about what you *won't* do. And God's Word contains very explicit instructions on what *not* to do.

For example, there is guidance about the specifics of *not:* losing your temper, expressing yourself in language which is not edifying, usurping someone's rightful authority, lying, cheating, or engaging in other behaviors which are clearly condemned in the Scriptures. But besides these specifics, there is one theme which asserts itself with powerful clarity: We must not, in any relationship, engage in any behavior which might harm us or someone else spiritually. The apostle Paul writes at great length about foregoing our own needs, desires, and rights in order to enhance the spiritual well-being of others.

But Jesus provides us with the most succinct, all-encompassing statement of what to consider when we are trying to decide what to do about an imperfect relationship for which there are no specific scriptural guidelines. "'There will always be temptations to sin,'" Jesus said one day to his disciples, "but woe to the man who does the tempting'" (Luke 17:1). Clearly, whatever our behavior, it must not provide occasion for another person to sin.

And now let's return to number 12 in the list of imperfect relationships. This is a real problem which occurs more frequently than many Christians would like to admit: Two Christians fall in love with each other, but one or both of them is married to someone else. This situation is ripe ground for great distress, especially if the love is mutual and reciprocated. What should be done?

In Chapter 1, two avenues for overcoming distress were identified: stress avoidance and stress management. Stress avoidance is the most desirable course of action to take, painful though it may be. But, sometimes it is too late for avoidance, or avoidance behaviors are not possible. Often one is already in an imperfect, bittersweet, male-female relationship, and it's impossible to predict where it will go. It becomes imperative, then, to remember that one does not have to know where a relationship *will* go, but where the relationship will *not* go. And for the Christian, it *cannot* go anywhere that it will:

1. Constitute a temptation to violate God's commandments;
2. Pose a threat to the spiritual development of self or others;
3. Present even the appearance of a bad example;
4. Distract from either individual's satisfaction with, or commitment to, his or her spouse.

There is, then, one way to overcome the stress of being in a relationship where male-female love is scripturally prohibited: Avoidance. The "management" steps are essentially "avoidance" steps.

If you have experienced this type of imperfect relationship, and if self-denial or the power to avoid is not readily available, ask God for his intervention in the relationship. He alone can make all things perfect, including *any* relationship.

Solving Imperfect Relationships: Facts That Can Help.
Fact: Only hermits are able to totally and consistently avoid imperfect interpersonal relationships.
Fact: Even if your personality is an exact duplicate of the personality of Jesus Christ, you have no guarantee that you can avoid imperfect interpersonal relationships. (Fact is, you might have more than your share! See 2 Timothy 3:12.)
Fact: Not all relationship problems are resolvable, even if scriptural guidelines are perfectly followed.
Fact: The stress of some problems in imperfect relationships can be avoided by following guidelines for interaction laid out in the Bible.
Fact: When an imperfect relationship is an unavoidable reality, stress can be managed by following God's instructions.

Sunday Dinner: Recipe for Indigestion

Many Christians have either experienced or heard about an after-church "Sunday dinner" which would look like this on a printed menu:

MENU
Sunday Dinner
Appetizers: Sour grapes and juicy tidbits of Hearsay
Main Dish: Roast pastor, Roast pastor's wife, or Roast fellow parishioner

All meals come with your choice of Sweet and Sour Comments, Instant Judgments, Half-baked Conclusions, and Spicy Morsels of Gossip, smothered in Criticism and well-stirred Simmering Envy.

Dessert: Humble Pie will eventually follow every meal.

Sound farfetched? Unfortunately many followers of Christ indulge in such bill of fare at home, at work, and at the homes of friends. The real or imagined shortcomings of supervisors, coworkers, family members, or strangers are served up as hors d'oeuvres. And once we succumb to the temptation of gossip and begin to nibble, the appetite for more substantial fare is stimulated until we become willing participants in the drawing, quartering, skewering, and roasting of our unsuspecting victims.

The chief problem of this kind of "meal" is that, at the very least, it always results in emotional indigestion for the "diners." At worst, it begins to create a craving for "junk food," for more of the same kind of slander, half truths, snide comments, pettiness, meanness, envy, and jealousy which were the basic ingredients of the original meal. Ultimately, it all has a destructive and weakening effect on the spirit, just as a steady diet of junk food would weaken the physical body.

These distress-inducing actions can be managed by following a number of avoidance guidelines.

Truth as a Guideline. "Always tell the truth, and you'll never have to remember what you said." Over one hundred and fifty years ago, Sir Walter Scott summarized in poetry the wisdom inherent in the prosaic quotation above. In 1808, he penned this oft-quoted couplet: "Oh, what a tangled web we weave, when first we practice to deceive!"

Whether it is stated in prose or in poetry, the lesson is clear: Distortion, lying, deceit, and other transgressions of the tongue ultimately result in situations which create distress. Many of our interpersonal and personal distresses are caused by an uncontrolled and undisciplined tongue.

These distresses were anticipated by the writers of the Scriptures who delineated guidelines for avoiding such problems. For example, the apostle James stressed the destructive forces of unbridled speech:

"Dear brothers, don't be too eager to tell others their faults, for we all make many mistakes; and when we teachers of religion, who should know better, do wrong, our punishment will be greater than it would be for others.

"If anyone can control his tongue, it proves that he has perfect control over himself in every other way. We can make a large horse turn around and go wherever we want by means of a small bit in his mouth. And a tiny rudder makes a huge ship turn wherever the pilot wants it to go, even though the winds are strong.

"So also the tongue is a small thing, but what enormous damage it can do. A great forest can be set on fire by one tiny spark. And the tongue is a flame of fire. It is full of wickedness and poisons every part of the body. And the tongue is set on fire by hell itself, and can turn our whole lives into a blazing flame of destruction and disaster.

"Men have trained, or can train, every kind of animal or bird that lives and every kind of reptile and fish, but no human being can tame the tongue. It is always ready to pour out its deadly poison. Sometimes it praises our heavenly Father, and sometimes it breaks out into curses against men who are made like God. And so blessing and cursing come pouring out of the same mouth. Dear brothers, surely this is not right!" (James 3:1-10).

Notice that James' admonition is concerned not only with the external destruction to others wreaked by the uncontrolled tongue. Our whole lives, James warns, can be turned into a blazing flame of destruction and disaster.

The same warning is stated in Colossians 3:9, and in Ephesians, when the apostle Paul explains with stirring simplicity that, "when we lie to each other, we are hurting ourselves" (Ephesians 4:25).

The distress-inducing potential of the uncontrolled tongue was regarded by the apostles as a grave danger. Not only the Ephesians, but the Corinthians, also, were a source of concern to Paul. He expressed his concern that, upon his return, he would find them "saying wicked things about each other and whispering behind each other's backs" (2 Corinthians 12:20).

So the first step in avoiding distress in relationships is to guard your tongue. (See James 3:1-10; Titus 3:2; 1 Peter 4:10.) Always keep in mind the main purpose of any communication you have: "And whatever you do or say, let it be as a representative of the Lord Jesus" (Colossians 3:17).

The menu for Sunday dinner included a dessert you can never refuse: humble pie. One way or another, an uncontrolled tongue will eventually humble its owner; one will have to "eat crow," or be faced with the responsibility for creating problems for himself or others through careless words.

Certain other behaviors in relationships also lead to self-created problems. Such things as jealousy, holding grudges, nursing hurt feelings, boasting, arguing, self-centeredness, and so on can lead to negative social, emotional, spiritual, and even physical effects. But God provides us with advice concerning each of these behaviors or qualities in his Word.

Look again at Keith's situation as it was discussed at the beginning of this chapter. He had been treated abusively and was suffering adverse consequences. Suppose he used the information and the avenues he had available to retaliate and "get even" with those abusing him. This action would only result in Keith victimizing *himself* with distress by:

1. Nursing his anger while he decides to act;
2. Chancing discovery as the source of the retaliatory action;

3. Taking the chance that his retaliation will not succeed, which would make him feel even more impotent and vulnerable than he was in the first place;

4. Bearing the burden of keeping his "success" to himself if he does get even, or bearing the subsequent burden of gossip after he tells "just one person" about his cleverness.

Most of us have faced times when we considered retaliating for some offense committed against us, if not for the world's reason that it would simply "feel good," then at least to "teach the person a lesson." Often, with a little imagination and rationalization, we conclude that the person who harmed us should be taught a lesson "for his own good."

If ever this rationale seemed perfectly logical, defensible, and reasonable, it would have been during the period immediately following the brutalization of the passengers and crew of hijacked TWA Flight 847 by Shi'ite fanatics in June 1985. The Shi'ite's savage disregard of even the most rudimentary appeals to morality was an outrage to the civilized world. They repeatedly beat the passengers and the crew of the flight with no provocation, and they viciously battered to death a young military man, callously dumping his body on the tarmac in Lebanon.

Their actions screamed for a retaliatory response by the United States government to teach the radical Shi'ite movement that terrorism against the people of the United States would not be tolerated. It was clear that moderation had not paid off; it had reaped only increased violence and had been interpreted by terrorist fanatics the world over as weakness. Those who experienced, even if only vicariously, the horror of abuse by terrorists, clamored for the United States to retaliate.

If any one person had reason to grit his teeth in fury and demand the full force of a U.S. military retaliation, it was Christian Zimmerman, the copilot and flight engineer on the ill-fated airplane. He had been restricted to the craft's hot, filthy confines for fifteen days. He had been repeatedly threatened and viciously assaulted. He had suffered emotional, spiritual, and physical abuse by grenade-juggling madmen who seemed to derive delight from their victims' impotent anxiety. And yet, Zimmerman publicly renounced any form of retaliation against his tormentors. In a testimony to his adherence to the teachings of Christ, Zimmerman had this to say on a radio talk show (which is hosted by one of the authors) about retaliation as national policy:

"I don't think it [retaliation] would be effective—in fact, I think it would be detrimental to . . . good relationships with any country . . . I believe when Jesus was speaking of turning the other cheek, he was suggesting a very practical solution as to how to end a bad or even a violent situation. If you can turn the other cheek, then it stops. Retaliation merely invites more counter-retaliation and then things just go on and on."

An amazing testimony from a man who suffered humiliation, indignities, and pain. Even more amazing were Zimmerman's gentle and patient responses to irate listeners who, in their frustration, called in to the show and suggested that he had been "taken in" by terrorist propaganda, or that he was an ignorant victim of his own naivete.

But Christian Zimmerman had clearly mastered the delayed negative effects of his stressful experience; he suffered acute stress—but in following Jesus' leading, he avoided *distress*. He mastered a major step in managing stress by applying God's insight into solving conflict.

Behavioral Guidelines. What does God say about "getting even," or about other stress-inducing, carnally-motivated behaviors? Well, God gives us a list of stress-reducing behaviors that looks like this:

Never Retaliate. Don't answer back when you're insulted. Don't threaten to get even. Don't snap back when people say unkind things to you. Leave your case in the hands of God; he will judge fairly and he will repay those who deserve it. The best way to respond to abusive treatment is with love and kindness. Go out of your way to show your concern and kindness to the people who are abusing you, and they will ultimately become ashamed of themselves for what they are doing to you.

If you follow these directives from God, in addition to the benefits of avoiding distress by letting God take care of your problem, you will also receive God's blessing for your nonretaliatory responses. (See Romans 12:19, 20; 13:14, 17; 1 Peter 3:9, 14, 23; 4:19.)

Never Nurse a Hurt, or Carry a Grudge. Think back to the last time that you nursed a hurt or carried a grudge. What words would you use to describe your feelings? Unlike instant anger, which *ex*plodes, prolonged grudges *im*plode—they exert a malignant force *inside* of us, creating a feeling which is far from positive. It is destructive, cold, and hard. And it produces distress.

God anticipated our capacity to nurse hurts and to carry grudges, and he knew their destructive side effects. So he provided this advice for us: "If you are angry, don't sin by nursing your grudge. Don't let the sun go down with you still angry—get over it quickly; for when you are angry you give a mighty foothold to the devil" (Ephesians 4:26, 27).

Avoid Arguments over Unimportant Things. Almost everyone knows of a situation in which people—sometimes even family members or in-laws—are not on speaking terms because of arguments over religion or politics. Invariably, hurt feelings and unretractable comments are all that is remembered; the original point of contention, that often was not significant in the first place, was forgotten long ago.

Insight into the dangers of argument for argument's sake—"foolish discussions" is Paul's terminology—provides the basis of a warning to Timothy, and to us, about the hurt feelings, the anger, and the smoldering resentment which result from such loveless debate. Paul is so acutely aware of the distressing results of a loveless argument that he goes to great lengths to provide advice on the topic in his letters to Timothy and Titus, and in his Epistle to the Romans. If a point is worth pursuing, Paul asserts in 2 Timothy 2:25, one's position should be asserted with kindness, gentleness, meekness, humility, and courtesy!

Another key to avoiding problems in relationships is to stay away from arguments over unanswerable theological questions. Satan stands ever ready to sow seeds of discord in the midst of even the most loving Christians. For example, some friends planned a hunting trip to New Mexico's high country. Mutual spiritual edification was intended to be a focal point of the trip. The trip had begun, in the planning stages months before, with prayer.

The first evening in the high country included the asking of the blessing before the evening meal, a repast which was enhanced by the pleasing aroma of a crackling piñon-fed campfire. The muffled murmurs of the night and the waning light of the blaze, whose flickering rays barely dispelled the awesomeness of the immense darkness of the wilderness, created an awareness in each man of the fact of his minuteness in

God's vast universe. It created a perfect aura for the Scripture reading intended to bless the men's camaraderie.

A quiet discussion of the Scripture could have been the perfect end to a perfect evening. But it wasn't. The discussion soon became pointed, then grew into a "friendly theological argument" over free will. They debated as though what had been studied and expounded upon for centuries was going to be resolved on a Friday night in a hunting camp in New Mexico! The friendly argument became less friendly and the older men cited Paul's admonition about argument—to no avail. The bright camaraderie of the early evening faded like the spent embers of the campfire.

Hours later, long after most of the members of the hunting party had retired for the night, the argument continued. Feelings were hurt, angry comments were exchanged. The barely camouflaged edge of insult intruded with bitter result. The spirit of the camp had been destroyed. For the principals and bystanders alike, the weekend was a distressing experience. But what was, perhaps, most distressing was the fact that had God's instructions been followed, the conflicts could have been totally avoided!

Redefine Your "Rights." We are accustomed to asserting our rights. A quick perusal of any major newspaper readily reveals the increasingly litigious nature of contemporary society. The call of "rights"—women's rights, students' rights, corporate rights, workers' rights, anyone's rights—readily evokes a militant response from an army of "rights" advocates ready to do battle for The Cause. It is only natural that Christians, too, have become imbued with the "rights" fervor. Natural, but not spiritual. What, exactly are the rights of Christians?

The undeniable and absolute rights of Christians are clearly specified in the Scriptures. They are here in "A Christian's Bill of Rights."

A Christian's Bill of Rights

Those who possess the gift of eternal life through faith in Jesus Christ as their Savior enjoy the following rights.

Article I
Each Christian has the right to "come fearlessly right into God's presence, assured of his glad welcome when we come with Christ and trust in him" (Ephesians 3:12), for "Christ has brought you into the very presence of God, and you are standing there before him with nothing left against you—nothing left that he could even chide you for" (Colossians 1:22).

Article II
As a Christian, you have the right to "let everything you do reflect your love of the truth, and the fact that you are in dead earnest about it" (Titus 2:7), and to "pray much for others; plead for God's mercy upon them; give thanks for all he is going to do for them" (1 Timothy 2:1).

As a Christian, you have the right to adopt those attitudes and behaviors that enhance the possibility of others accepting Jesus Christ as their Savior. (See Romans 14; 15:1-3; and 1 Corinthians 3:3.)

Article III
As a Christian, you have the right to "try to please everyone in everything [you] do, not doing what [you] like or what is best for [you], but what is best for them, so they may be saved" (1 Corinthians 10:33).

Article IV
As a Christian, you have the right to "think of the other fellow, too, and what is best for him" (1 Corinthians 10:24).

Article V
As a Christian, you have the right to "be humble, thinking of others as better than yourself" (Philippians 2:3).

Article VI
As a Christian, you have the right to experience opportunities to win people for Christ throughout your life. (See Philippians 1:20, 21.)

Article VII
As a Christian, you have the right to "practice tenderhearted mercy and kindness to others" and to "be ready to suffer quietly and patiently" (Colossians 3:12).

Article VIII
As a Christian you have the right to be "the world's seasoning, to make it tolerable" (Matthew 5:13).

Article IX
As a Christian, you have the right to take a stand on the side of good. (See Romans 12:9, 10.)

Article X
As a Christian, you have the right to "try to show as much compassion as your Father does" (Luke 6:36).

Now, how does a set of such behaviors translate into
stress reduction (or better yet, distress-avoidance) in
interpersonal relationships? Simply like this: If a person
is totally dedicated to serving Christ through serving
others, his main concern is the response of other people
to the Gospel of Christ, and his main goal becomes
putting the rights of others over his own rights! "For
even I, the Messiah," Jesus declared, "am not here to be
served, but to help others, and to give my life as a
ransom for many" (Mark 10:45).

Shall it then be concluded that Christians should be
"door mats"? Quite the contrary! The example of Paul's
insistence on his rights in Philippi, after he and Silas
had been unlawfully imprisoned and punished,
provides an example of when insistence on one's secular
rights is a desirable course of action. In demanding his
right, as a Roman citizen, to public exoneration and a
public apology from his persecutors, Paul established a
climate in which Christians were much less likely to be
harassed for preaching the Gospel than they might have
been had he meekly submitted to injustice. The criterion
is clear: *You have a right to determine whether to assert
your rights or whether to forego your rights solely on the
basis of whether your decision serves the Gospel of Jesus
Christ!* (See Titus 2:7; 3:14; 1 Peter 3:17 and 2 Peter 1:6,
7.)

Forget about "Impressions." The criterion that guides the
asserting of rights is the same criterion advocated by
God for determining how we interact with others.
Many people have tried so hard to make a good
impression—to be genuinely warm, interested, and
friendly—that they created the impression of being
artificial, disinterested, and preoccupied.

There is an intriguing story about impressions that
goes like this: Two people meet, and the first individual
shows great interest in the other person. He elicits
from him anecdote after anecdote about his interests,

successes, and achievements. Hours pass and the second person animatedly continues his narrative, while his listener provides rapt attention. Later, in the privacy of his home, the storyteller confides to his wife: "I met the most interesting person this evening . . ." and is startled to discover, in response to his wife's query, that he knows nothing at all about his new acquaintance. The fact is, what was most interesting about the evening was that someone had expressed genuine interest in him!

This principle of successful interpersonal interaction was first stated in the Scriptures: "Don't just think about your own affairs, but be interested in others too, and in what they are doing" (Philippians 2:4).

The apostle Paul extends this admonition in the same chapter: "Don't be selfish; don't live to make a good impression on others" (Philippians 2:3).

Concern about enhancing our own image or our own reputation will always lead to distress. First, we will be more concerned about how we are coming across than about being "salt." We will begin to be silent when we should speak up; to straddle issues rather than take a side. We will suffer the constant tension of trying to determine the situation and how we have to adapt, rather than experience the confident certainty that we live to please Christ, not man.

Imagine the distress you might feel if you tried to establish your credibility and credentials in public and someone brazenly and openly criticized you. You would feel embarrassed and uncomfortable. But these feelings of distress would not be so strong if you had Christ's attitude. He experienced a public denunciation and responded with confidence. His declaration transcended the situation and pointed toward a higher standard: "Your approval or disapproval means nothing to me, for as I know so well, *you don't have God's love within you*" (John 5:41, 42, italics added). Notice Jesus' criterion for determining whether someone's approval was worth striving for. The lesson is clear. We should relate to others to advance the Gospel, and we have God's promise of the help of the Holy Spirit in that endeavor. Then we will suffer no stress.

Conversely, when we relate to others to advance ourselves, we try to meet inappropriate criteria. Whether we are accepted or rejected, we suffer distress. We have lost sight of our real purpose.

Choose Your Friends and Associates Carefully. Imagine a powerfully-muscled, thick-necked Belgian draft horse. It stands almost six feet high at the shoulder, weighs one and a half tons, and is the product of a species that has been bred over the centuries for massive strength. Its size is overwhelming, the extent of its power awesome. Standing next to it is a Shetland pony, three and a half feet tall, doubly dwarfed in comparison. Imagine the ensuing chaos if the Belgian and the Shetland were harnessed as a team! No amount of outside help, no extra training, no readjustment of load, no encouragement, and least of all, no good intentions, could even remotely hope to get this unequally yoked team to pull as well as two Belgians, or, for that matter, even as well as two Shetland ponies.

Second Corinthians 6:14, 15 portrays exactly this scene for us, warning Christians of the dangers inherent in "teaming up with" or becoming a partner in friendship, marriage, business, or in any way with non-Christians:

"Don't be teamed with those who do not love the Lord, for what do the people of God have in common with the people of sin? How can light live with darkness? And what harmony can there be between Christ and the devil? How can a Christian be a partner with one who doesn't believe?"

Distress is certain to result in such relationships. But

the analogy of the horses is incomplete. In order to fully illustrate Paul's point, one of the horses would be facing in one direction, and the other animal facing in the opposite direction. For not only are Christians and non-Christians *inherently* different, they are striving for different goals!

Don't Make Comparisons with Others. Don't make comparisons, and don't let anyone impose comparisons, explicit or implicit, upon you. Why not? Because if God is the source of everything about you, then your comparison with others of what you possess or what you have achieved is pointless. God gives what he wants to whomever he chooses (Ephesians 4:7), and every ability from God is a necessary ability, a part of the body (Ephesians 4:12). Comparisons are both pointless and logically indefensible. Only an irrational person would pursue such an action.

The Scriptures state that comparisons lead to distress; that self-aggrandizement produces negative emotions (see Galatians 5:26). The Scriptures further teach that you should evaluate your achievements by the extent to which your "best" was pursued. "Let everyone be sure that he is doing his very best," Paul says in Galatians 6:4, "for then he will have the personal satisfaction of work well done, and won't need to compare himself with someone else."

Paul's advice is a formula for satisfaction. It's a formula for avoiding the distresses of anxiety, envy, jealousy, or covetousness when those with whom we compete seem to be receiving all the accolades, achieving all the quotas, creating the best ideas, or just plain leaving us behind.

And the distress of unfavorably comparing oneself with another is an inescapable reality, one which has given rise to the caustic cynicism of such adages as C. C. Colton's observation, "If you want enemies, excel others; if you want friends, let others excel you."

A Christian's criterion for evaluation of actions is simple: Am I doing my best? If so, I can relax and be satisfied. For if "I seek to honor God with my efforts" (John 7:18), then he will bless my efforts. I have an *internal*, God-sanctified standard of evaluation.

Be a Friend. We've all encountered the stranger who accidently catches our eye, who does not want to appear unfriendly, and who, therefore, comes up with that all-too-familiar, lips-together, corners-of-mouth-barely-upturned "almost smile," which conveys, if not friendliness, at least an absence of hostility. You've seen it; it almost makes it into a smile, but not quite. A real smile might be too forward or it might evoke no response or a quizzical look—or rejection. So the stranger doesn't smile. And we don't smile.

Neither do we, with the exception of a few super gregarious souls, extend the hand of friendship. We are shy, withdrawn, afraid of people. But what does God say?

"For the Holy Spirit, God's gift, does not want you to be afraid of people, but to be wise and strong, and to love them and enjoy being with them" (2 Timothy 1:7).

What else does God say about being a friend?

"The one who serves you best will be your leader" (Luke 27:26).

"When others are happy, be happy with them. If they are sad, share their sorrow" (Romans 12:15).

"Work happily together . . . and don't think you know it all" (Romans 12:16).

"If you love someone . . . you will always believe in him, always expect the best of him, and always stand your ground in defending him" (1 Corinthians 13:7).

"*Say only what is good and helpful to those you are talking to, and what will give them a blessing*" (Ephesians 4:29).

"*[Avoid] dirty stories, foul talk, and coarse jokes*" (Ephesians 5:4).

"*Work hard and with gladness all the time*" (Ephesians 6:6, 7).

"*Stay away from complaining and arguing*" (Philippians 2:14).

"*Honor [those] who work hard among you*" (1 Thessalonians 5:12).

"*Warn those who are lazy; comfort those who are frightened; take tender care of those who are weak; and be patient with everyone*" (1 Thessalonians 5:14).

"*[See] goodness and purity in everything*" (Titus 1:15).

"*Let us outdo each other in being helpful and kind*" (Hebrews 10:24).

It is unarguable that a person who possesses the qualities listed above would be eagerly sought as a friend. Striving to incorporate these qualities will greatly improve your interpersonal relationships.

The scriptural advice on avoiding stress in interpersonal relationships can be accepted readily if one is totally committed to his major purpose in life: advancing the Gospel of Christ. Total commitment to this goal means that, with the Holy Spirit's leading, we can work to guard our tongues, never retaliate, never nurse a hurt or carry a grudge, avoid arguments, redefine our rights, forget about impressions, choose our friends and associates carefully, avoid comparisons with others, and be a godly friend.

But even if we closely follow the Scriptures, we won't be able to completely avoid imperfect relationships. The poison of sin is always there to contaminate relationships and create distress, even among Christians. Because of this unavoidable contamination, we must learn to *manage* relationships in ways that are edifying both to others and ourselves and that are glorifying to God.

Managing Imperfect Relationships
The board of directors advised him to sue. After all, a solid commitment had been made to him. His time, talents, and personal finances had been expended based on that commitment. The property for Kids for Christ Ranch, the culmination of a dream for Richard Rader that had begun three years earlier (a dream to which he had devoted all of his energies and tens of thousands of dollars of his own money), had been donated to Rader's foundation.

His burden for abused children had begun with a "chance" experience in Los Angeles, California. A friend had been involved in an official capacity in a case of child abuse. What had been, in the past, an abstract social problem to Richard Rader now became an instant and horrifying reality, one that he would devote his life to correcting.

Knowing nothing of regulations, restrictions, licensing, red tape, expenses, and numerous related details, Rader gave up his work as an independent oil producer and set out to establish a ranch for abused children. Miraculously, after months of arduous effort, a benefactor donated a beautiful site, complete with buildings, above the Grand Mesa near Grand Junction, Colorado. It was, in Richard's mind, the perfect haven for suffering children. He was completely dedicated to the ranch and grateful to the benefactor.

And then the dream became a nightmare. Just as suddenly as the ranch had been given, the offer was rescinded. There was a difference in perception between the benefactor and Richard Rader. Each perceived the other to be wrong, but the legal opinion shared at the board of directors' meeting was that the case could be won in court by Richard Rader. At the most, the ranch—tangible manifestation of the dream to which Rader had devoted his life—would remain under his control. At the least, he would recover close to twenty-five thousand dollars of his personal expenses spent in improvements to the ranch and endeavors related to the ranch.

But the ranch and the foundation were, after all, Kids for *Christ* Ranch, which implied, with no room for equivocation, that *Christ* would be honored in seeking a solution. And where better to seek a solution than in the Scriptures? What, Richard wondered, did the Scriptures say about resolving such problems, and what did Christ say about lawsuits?

Consider, now, the stress in this situation. The benefactor, motivated by good intentions, suffered the stress of wrestling with his decision to withdraw his offer, and the anxiety of potentially facing a costly lawsuit. He was apprehensive about the reaction of the board—a board before which he had expressed a public commitment. Richard, on the other hand, grappled to manage the stress of the loss of his personal resources, and, even more significantly, with the loss of a dream to which he had made a total commitment. How could he save his dream and resources and not end up in a bitter relationship with a Christian brother, the owner of the ranch?

Fortunately for everyone, the problem-solving guidelines of the Scriptures were sought, and the advice of the board was ignored. Richard discovered that a follower of Jesus is primarily concerned with enhancing the preaching of the Gospel of Christ—that is, honoring Christ; enhancing the spiritual well-being of his brother or sister in Christ; and enhancing his own spiritual well-being. This set of criteria from the Scriptures convinced the board of Kids for Christ Ranch and Richard Rader to follow Jesus' instructions for solving such a problem:

"If a brother sins against you, go to him privately and confront him with his fault. If he listens and confesses it, you have won back a brother. But if not, then take one or two others with you and go back to him again, proving everything you say by these witnesses. If he still refuses to listen, then take your case to the church, and if the church's verdict favors you, but he won't accept it, then the church should excommunicate him" (Matthew 18:15-17).

Since Rader and the board considered finding a solution to this problem in the civil courts, they also sought and found Scripture guidelines concerning such actions:

"How is it that when you have something against another Christian, you 'go to law' and ask a heathen court to decide the matter instead of taking it to other Christians to decide which of you is right? Don't you know that some day we Christians are going to judge and govern the world? So why can't you decide even these little things among yourselves? Don't you realize that we Christians will judge and reward the very angels in heaven? So you should be able to decide your problems down here on earth easily enough. Why then go to outside judges who are not even Christians? I am trying to make you ashamed. Isn't there anyone in all the church who is wise enough to decide these arguments? But, instead, one Christian sues another and accuses his Christian brother in front of unbelievers.

"To have such lawsuits at all is a real defeat for you as Christians. Why not just accept mistreatment and leave it at that? It would be far more honoring to the Lord to let yourselves be cheated" (1 Corinthians 6:1-7).

An ultimate solution to the problem was reached, though it was not a solution which completely satisfied Richard Rader, who gave up some of his "rights." Nor did it completely satisfy the ranch's former benefactor, who also gave up some of his "rights." It *was*, however, a solution which satisfied God's guidelines and commands. For each man had been motivated by a principle higher than the principle of rights. Each man had "lost" something material, but each man had gained a brother. Each man experienced stress, but in faithfully following God's command, neither of them experienced distress.

The Kids for Christ story and the God-pleasing way in which the problem was solved was a particularly edifying experience for one of the authors, who was one of the "one or two others" mentioned by Jesus as an integral part of the problem-solving method in Matthew 18. But what happens when Matthew 18 is followed and one of the following circumstances is encountered?

1. The person who has hurt you is a Christian, but there is no "church" as such to whose authority each of you submits, thereby rendering "taking it to the church" impossible.
2. The person who has hurt you is or is not a Christian, and he or she totally misconstrues your loving intent, verbally assails you, subsequently distorts the substance and climate of what you intended as a loving encounter, and thereafter refuses to speak to you or to a mediating third party.
3. Nobody has sinned against you, but you know that somebody has something against you, and you want to follow Jesus' advice in Matthew 5: "So if you are standing before the altar in the Temple, offering a sacrifice to God, and suddenly remember that a friend has something against you, leave your sacrifice there beside the altar and go and apologize and be reconciled to him, and then come and offer your sacrifice to God" (vv. 23, 24).

But when you go to the person, he responds to your peaceful overture with a hostile or ungracious rebuff. You now find yourself in the unenviable position of having exposed yourself. You wanted to honor God and "win" a brother, but instead you have made yourself vulnerable to an "enemy." Before, he could only conjecture about your knowledge of his feelings; now he knows you are no longer innocently and naively ignorant. Because of this, you may now pose a threat to him, and he may seek the opportunity for a vindictive response.

What do you do? Jesus provides answers for all of these situations.

Illogical Instructions: Logical Outcomes. Nowhere in the Scriptures does the Word of God promise that, if one "turns the other cheek," it, too, won't be slapped. Or that, if one "goes the extra mile," he won't be forced to walk yet another mile. And when the Book of Proverbs declares that, "When a man is trying to please God, God makes even his worst enemies to be at peace with him" (Proverbs 16:7), the lessons of the total Scripture imply an interpretation that one's enemies will not be able to make a valid case against him, not that they won't make false accusations against him.

Obviously, we live in a world controlled by Satan, who deals in deceit, duplicity, lies, and vindictiveness— the full array of aspersive and destructive carnal inclinations. And those who have not personally submitted themselves to the will of the Son of God are all too eager to slap the other cheek, to seize the cloak and the coat, and to demand yet another mile. As the Scripture clearly warns—they will stop at nothing (see Romans 1:31). What do we do when we have to deal with these people? Here is what Jesus says:

"But I say: Love your enemies! Pray for those who persecute you!" (Matthew 5:44).
"Listen, all of you. Love your enemies. Do good to those who hate you. Pray for the happiness of those who curse you; implore God's blessing on those who hurt you" (Luke 6:27, 28).

This perplexing advice seems totally irrational and contrary to what we might hope for, namely, that our enemies will be cursed and that they will be miserably unhappy! But let's do a little logical analysis. If our enemies are *cursed*, then: (1) they will not be responsive to God; so (2) they won't be guided by God's love; therefore (3) they must be guided by Satan, who seeks to harm Christians; which means (4) our enemies will only seek to harm us more fervently; and (5) we will ultimately be faced with negative stress.

Let's take the analysis a little further. If we pray for our enemies' unhappiness, then: (1) they will be miserable, bitter, and angry; and (2) they will seek someone to blame for their unhappiness or someone upon whom they can vent their unhappiness; and (3) they will be more difficult to deal with than ever; which probably means that (4) we become likely candidates for their anger, and a target of their vindictiveness; which means (5) we once again face a great deal of negative stress.

Now let's look at Jesus' seemingly illogical approach. If we implore God's blessing upon our enemies, this means that the Holy Spirit will begin to work upon their hearts, for God's greatest blessing to anyone is the Holy Spirit, who leads to faith in Christ. If this happens—but a total step-by-step analysis isn't necessary, is it? Because once our enemies are blessed by God's Holy Spirit, they will be incapable of dealing with us in any way other than in the love of Christ!

Therefore, it makes eminently good sense to implore God's blessings upon our enemies. When someone is so blessed, he will not consciously create negative stress. Rather he becomes a source of positive reinforcement!

The same God-pleasing, Christ-honoring result is achieved when we follow Jesus' admonition to pray for the happiness of our enemies. For even if our enemies do not become brothers or sisters in Christ, we have at least taken steps to diffuse the impact of their hostility. Our enemies are more likely to direct an assault on us when they are unhappy. To minimize the probability of having to manage negative stress, then, it only makes sense to follow the wisdom of God and pray for our enemies' happiness.

. . . And After All, Are You Really Vulnerable? He stood in apparently defenseless vulnerability, his wrists cruelly chafed by the tightly-bound restraints, his lips split by repeated blows to the mouth, his nostrils caked with dried blood, and his face swollen and raw from hours of unprovoked torture. And now the one man who could set him free was shouting at him in frustration: "'You won't talk to me?' Pilate demanded. 'Don't you realize that I have the power to release you or to crucify you?' Then Jesus said, 'You would have no power at all over me unless it were given to you from above . . .'" (John 19:10, 11).

Jesus, not Pilate, was in control of the situation, for he knew, without doubt, that God was in control.

Scripture is full of encouragement to Christians who live in an evil world. Regardless of our apparent vulnerability to this evil, it is God who controls our lives, and who directs our paths (see Proverbs 3:5, 6; and Romans 8:25-28). God turns others' evil intentions around to work for our best interests (see Genesis 50:20; Romans 8:38). He has the power to alter the minds of our adversaries, to direct their thoughts toward us (Ezra 1:1; 7:6; Nehemiah 1:11; and Proverbs 21:1; 29:26).

God promises us: *"There is no need to fear when times of trouble come,* even though surrounded by enemies" (Psalm 49:5).

Summary
This chapter has outlined steps for the avoidance of distress in imperfect relationships, and for the managing of the stress of imperfect relationships. But whole volumes have been written about specific interpersonal problems, such as raising children, healing wounded marital relationships, and coping with chemically dependent loved ones. The steps outlined in this book can help you to avoid or to solve many such problems, but their complexity requires in-depth treatment. (For this reason, Appendix A includes a bibliography of sources which have proven helpful in managing the many and varied stresses of imperfect interpersonal relationships.)

Remember the prayer at the beginning of the chapter? "Lord, help me to pray for others at least as often as I am tempted to criticize them." It implies two major keys in interpersonal relationships: Pray for others often (including your enemies) and guard your speech.

Following these keys, and the principles derived from God's Word, will have positive results because, unlike secular theories evolved from hypothesizing and postulating, they are based on the insights provided in the Word of God.

Seven
Uncommon Sense about Dollars: Managing Financial Stress

Butter: Sixty Thousand Dollars a Pound

In the months, weeks, and days preceding the cataclysmic collapse of the German economy in 1923, the emotional distress caused by fear of what *might* happen was as inescapable as the stress of the actual events. Disaster was imminent; anxiety was pervasive.

Potatoes, which had sold for about one tenth of a mark per pound in 1918, cost eighty marks per pound in 1922. Butter, which could be purchased for three marks per pound in 1918, cost two thousand four hundred marks per pound in early 1922, and one hundred and fifty thousand marks—over sixty thousand American dollars at current rates of exchange—by summer of 1922!

For both the upper and lower economic classes, there was an awareness that the external forces of commerce affecting them defied not only control, but explanation. These same forces are equally uncontrollable and inexplicable over half a century later. It is a grim, inescapable reality that they possess the potential to threaten the economic security of individuals and of nations.

Even the most shrewd and judicious investor is vulnerable to the unpredictable impulses of commerce. Historical hedges against the inflation that destroyed

German economy are pitifully insecure. Diamonds seemed an attractive investment in 1980, at a high price of sixty-four thousand dollars for a top-grade, one-carat stone. But in early 1985, this "sure-fire" hedge against inflation had plummeted to an unanticipated, startlingly low price of twelve thousand. At the same time, the financial alliance of the OPEC countries, which had been unamenable to the maneuverings of the industrial powers and unsympathetic to the plight of developing nations, crumbled from within. It became a victim of the unpredictable financial instability of several of its member nations.

Clearly, no individual, group, nation, or group of nations is immune to financial stress.

A Pot of Nothing at the End of the Rainbow. It was to be the first privately financed Olympic Games ever. Corporate giants scrambled to enter the bidding arena, hoping to be labeled "the official this" or "the official that" of the U. S. Olympic Team. Everything that could be marketed with an official "Olympics" association insignia was produced, packaged, and promoted to eager throngs as the 1984 Olympic Games in Los Angeles were launched. It was capitalism at its best: Millions of hearts swelled with long-dormant national pride and patriotic fervor as Old Glory was unfurled and the cymbals crashed to herald each new American conquest. "U.S.A., U.S.A.!" The chant rolled through the crowds so that even the newscasters caught, or perhaps fostered, the blossoming of a new national consciousness.

The thrill of achievement was undeniable; the identification factor irresistible. And merchandising in association with the Olympics became a paying proposition. Entrepreneurs, both individual and corporate, stood to reap handsome profits. The right combination of patriotic ingredients could be worth millions.

One logo, the "Baseball U.S.A." logo, became that right combination. It had it all: baseball, the uniquely American sport; the colors of red, white, and blue; the bold, and dominating "U.S.A."; and the flag whose red bars and shooting stars swooped from the tail of the all-American sport, hovering in a protective half-embrace over the letters "U.S.A." It was the perfect logo.

It seemed to move with fluidity and power as it graced the uniforms of the U.S. Olympic team. It commanded attention on thousands of letterheads, posters, and pieces of advertising of the United States Baseball Federation. Here was graphic gold for the creative artist from whose drawing board the design had sprung! Think of it—royalties from thousands of T-shirts, decals, posters, and other Olympic mementos. The pride of achievement and of being acknowledged. It was a once-in-a-lifetime opportunity!

But the fact of a possible fortune had not been immediately obvious to Doug Bliss. In 1981, graphic artists in Colorado were not in demand. Some, including Doug, were struggling at the minimum wage level. Doug was barely making it. He was thirty years old, he had a wife and two children, and his job at a small independent sporting goods store provided only a precarious existence. Even with food stamps there was not enough to eat. "We had to give our situation to the Lord," Doug said, recalling his struggle for the economic survival of his family.

And then came the logo. With his mind preoccupied with problems of basic survival, Doug responded to a casual request. When the United States Baseball Federation had scheduled a meeting at the University of Northern Colorado, someone had asked Doug to come up with a baseball logo. He did so, and there were the usual gratuitous expressions of approval, but nothing more. USBF departed, and the conference ended, as did conversation about the logo. The whole episode was not really forgotten, since it had never had much significance to Doug in the first place. It was simply not remembered. Then came the shock—the flood of confused surprise, and speculation. Doug's employer had received a piece of bulk mail—a standard form letter—from the United States Baseball Federation. And there, leaping from the envelope and emblazoned across the top of the letter inside was Doug's logo: Baseball U.S.A.! What could this possibly mean? What were the ramifications?

Like a high school freshman flushed with his first varsity assignment, Doug raced home to share with Jeanne his eager anticipation of the positive potential which danced on the horizon. He lacked the experience to anticipate in specifics, but he did know that this was good—great, even! The store owner made preliminary contact with the USBF. What benefits would accrue to the graphic artist? No direct response was forthcoming, but it was announced that baseball would be a demonstration sport in the '84 Olympics! For Doug, there would be Olympic "gold" in "Baseball U.S.A."!

This brainchild, conceived in the midst of his young family's desperate financial plight, promised to catapult Doug's family to virtually instant affluence. The need to ask God for daily bread would be left behind. "Baseball U.S.A.," the logo on the uniforms of the United States Olympic baseball team, which would later be seen on international television by millions of spectators, was a natural for commercial exploitation.

Now it was 1985. Doug Bliss, no longer dependent

upon food stamps but still occupied with adequately providing daily bread, described his thoughts and emotions during the past several years: "I received absolutely nothing from my design of the 'Baseball U.S.A.' logo. . . . I don't understand what happened . . . it was some kind of 'right' they had to it, I guess. All I know is that after I submitted it, it was used."

Doug's voice trailed off. He sat quietly for a moment, his eyes unconsciously scrutinizing the wall of his workroom, as though pensively seeking some window to the past which would show a specific moment at which he lost ownership of his "Baseball U.S.A." logo and the tremendous financial rewards that went with it.

Finally I broke in. "So you got no money, and no glory. Weren't you frustrated? Don't you feel bitter when you think about this once-in-a-lifetime opportunity being grabbed away? Haven't you thought about legal action? You seem incredibly calm about this."

I couldn't understand Doug's passivity. But earlier in our conversation, he had related how he and his wife had come to an acute awareness of what was meant by "*daily* bread."

"Jeanne and I came to the point where we thought, 'If we have something to eat *tonight*, that's fine.' We just trusted God for our daily bread—not our *monthly* bread. We knew it was a promise."

So there he sat, bent over his drawing board, still struggling to make a living. Yet he seemed at total peace despite the chain of events that would have evoked self-pity, anger, aggression, frustration, and bitter cynicism in most other people.

I rephrased my question. "What are your feelings now, Doug, since times are still tough for you, and you haven't received any recognition or financial reward?"

Doug's words, like his demeanor, reinforced the peace of mind he conveyed. "I do believe in fairness and a reward somewhere if it is to be. I'm comfortable with what happened. I'm not sitting back; I believe in the grind and hard work. You have to 'change characters'—you know, change your nature to protect yourself," he asserted. "I find it hard to do. I played it straight the whole way. I didn't complain; I did my part. And God will do his part. If I had been paid for 'Baseball U.S.A.,' if I had had that success—Jeanne and I would not be where we are today, spiritually. Besides, I know that real success comes from God."

"But what about the stress, Doug?" I interrupted, still amazed by his calm acceptance and resolute faith. "Don't you feel *any* stress about how the USBF and others have used your designs and not compensated you?"

"God needed to take the hard road to develop me spiritually," was Doug's response. "I hope he keeps doing it. After seeing many of God's promises fulfilled through all of this, I expect other promises to be fulfilled."

If the 1988 Olympics are held, as scheduled, in South Korea, where baseball is a popular sport, baseball will receive unprecedented attention throughout the world. But the commanding "Baseball U.S.A." logo will do much more than identify the American team. It will provide brilliant witness to a young artist's absolute trust in the sovereignty and faithfulness of his God, who provided him with both his creative ability and his daily bread.

From Riches to Rags: The Survival of Kennie Anderson. Two and a half million dollars of net worth more than compensated for a lack of height. By his own admission, Kennie Anderson, at five feet, five inches tall, "used to get power and lose inferiority by riding herd on others." And with twenty-one employees under his supervision, there was plenty of room to ride herd. He was domineering, combative, proud, and aggressive. A self-made man, Kennie had, in twenty years, parlayed two hundred and sixty-two dollars and a cutting torch into a recycling operation with an annual volume of millions of dollars. From 1962 until 1982, he couldn't miss.

"I was lucky and wealthy," he mused. "Everything I touched turned to gold." When had he felt like a success? he was asked. "From the very beginning," he declared. "I couldn't do a thing wrong. I even had my name on the honor roll at church. I was fourth in giving," he reminisced, an embarrassed half-smile creeping to his face. "I was a great churchgoer. But as far as being a Christian, I didn't know what the word meant."

His success, his apparent generosity, and his obvious business acumen did not go unnoticed. Even though Kennie, who became a forty-year-old, self-made millionaire, did not know a thing about Jesus Christ, he received invitations to serve on two Christian governing boards. And he attended Christian fellowship meetings. His social interests were many and diverse. His financial interests—holdings in silver bullion, property, and a tremendous inventory—were equally diversified. And it was all paying off.

Then there came a turn of events totally foreign to Kennie's experience or to his expectations. First were the accidents—a bad automobile collision, and then, a few months later, a flipped-over semi-trailer which skidded off an icy road. But some of his luck had held; he could have been killed, the paramedics told him. The possibility of death had never occurred to him. But now there was an awareness—a distressing discomfort—that death was an unpredictable inevitability. Kennie continued to associate with Christians, out of habit. And God continued to smile upon him.

Kennie's conversion and its timing were God-inspired. His accidents, the distressing awareness of his vulnerability to death, his association with Christians, and the touching faith of a wizened old man in a nursing home who pierced Kennie's heart with a moving prayer on Christmas Eve in 1980, all joined to result in Kennie's committing his life to Christ in October of the following year. But it would only be much later that Kennie would appreciate how significant the timing of his commitment really was.

The first hint of this came when the market in aluminum, which had been the flagship of his recycling empire, sagged. In November 1981, at sixty-five cents a pound, it sold for less than what he had paid for it. He had been a Christian for exactly one month. By December, the market plummeted to forty-five cents a pound, and a month later, it thudded to an all-time low of forty cents a pound.

And then, the unheard-of—Kennie Anderson could not sell, at any price, even one pound of aluminum. And what at first had been only a vaguely discernible slip in selling prices on the rest of Kennie's inventory became a massive slide. Pueblo's CF and I Steel, a major corporate customer that had measured their orders in railroad car quantities, cancelled all orders.

The erosion of Kennie's financial holdings, which had begun with the disaster in aluminum, continued. Diversification, the investment strategy that had had such a solid sound to it, suddenly dissolved into an empty, hollow echo. What all the financial wizards had told him would be a defense against inflation or recession, dissolved. An internationally repercussive crash in the price of silver assailed not only Kennie Anderson, but professional investment groups as well.

The financial avalanche threatened to pull Kennie into a dark vortex of despair. He was battered by problems and circumstances he had never even remotely anticipated. There was fear and dissension among his employees; layoffs became necessary. His financial resources were exhausted. His inventory was heavily amortized. The economic giant who had stood astride a twenty-eight acre empire, riding herd on twenty-one intimidated employees, now straddled an ever-widening gap between assets and liabilities. Soon Kennie was bowed with the burden of a quarter of a million dollar debt at 21 percent interest. He recounted his emotional turmoil:

"I couldn't believe what had happened and how fast it had happened. I had to lay off a third of my employees in only four months. My wife and I were down to six hundred dollars, and I had no salary coming in. In fact, I had worked day in and day out for seven months without even one paycheck. It was like a nightmare. I would go home after work, and my wife and I would fight constantly. Money was a constant thorn in our sides. I would wake up at three or four in the morning, feeling as though hungry employees and a quarter million dollar debt were pushing on my body, pressing in on me. I would get up in the darkness and try to figure out how to meet just one more day's expenses. You see, you have to understand," Kennie unflinchingly confessed, "money was my god. I had thought it was impossible for me to go down the tubes."

A succinct and cynical observation on human nature is found in the conclusion of the second chapter of the Gospel of John. Jesus, John confides, didn't trust the crowds, although many were proclaiming him as the Messiah. "He knew mankind to the core. No one needed to tell him how changeable human nature is!" (John 2:24, 25). And Kennie Anderson was soon to be made painfully aware of this.

As his business foundered, he became an object of hatred for many of his employees. He was accused behind his back of hiding company assets and cheating his employees. Longtime friends deserted him. Acquaintances, eager to wallow in the mud of ugly rumor, turned their backs on him. Business associates, quick to disclaim responsibility for the disastrous economic forecasts they had asserted only months before, now urged Kennie to bite the bullet, take his lumps, and declare bankruptcy.

But Kennie Anderson did not stand alone. "As black as things got," he said, "Romans 8:31 kept coming through. 'What can we ever say to such wonderful things as these? If God is on our side, who can ever be against us?' And there were Christians who encouraged me, helped me, and prayed for me. Everybody else told me to hang it up, but the Christians knew what they were talking about. 'Stay in there,' they'd say. 'God loves you.' So I kept thinking about Romans 8:31. I was only a new Christian, but I believed that God would take care of me, no matter what."

God's care exceeded Kennie's expectations. "I didn't know or realize the power of prayer then," Kennie admitted. "But I know it today." Conviction asserted itself in Kennie's voice. "Today, I am back to full 100 percent in my employees. My business is completely out of the red. Our volume is again measured in the millions. And I'm richer in other ways, because I have a different attitude toward people. I have more compassion for people who are hurting. And I don't have to compensate for my height anymore. I feel complete and worthwhile in Jesus Christ. I just hope that hearing about my experiences will help other people trust in God when they face a financial crisis."

Financial Stress in the Corporate World. The economic fairy tale called "Storage Tek" had ended, abruptly. It was a casualty of the lender's refusal of a one hundred and fifty million dollar transfusion. The once aggressive, worldwide, Fortune 500 Company that had generated a multimillion dollar annual payroll was now struggling with Chapter Eleven bankruptcy. Thousands of stunned employees from assembly line workers to managers, faced a bleak future. At Storage Technology's Colorado plant alone, over four thousand people would ultimately suffer layoffs.

The advance awareness, however, had done nothing to cushion the aftershock of the cutbacks. Perhaps it was the continuous tension caused by two years of layoffs, or by the mounting anxiety of watching steadily growing unsold inventory. Whatever it was, plant security was increased as more layoffs were announced. But the stress, which had been valiantly controlled for months, finally exploded in violence. Fistfights broke out first in the parking lots, then in the plants themselves.

"I was told," one supervisor recalled, "that in our sister plant, one of our engineers collapsed right in his office when informed of the loss of his job. Another executive's bleeding ulcer flared up, and he was taken to the hospital in critical condition. There were threats against management and against coworkers, and security was increased, because they suspected sabotage. They destroyed lives there."

Destroyed lives—an all-too-common result of acute distress over economic survival.

The "What If" and the "What Is" of Stress
There are two types of financial stress mentioned in the Scriptures: *emotion-generated* stress and *event-generated* stress. Emotion-generated stress is inside stress from worrying about what might happen ("What if . . ."). Event-generated stress is outside stress, or stress in response to what is taking place around us. Whichever stress we experience, unless we learn solid stress management techniques, the results will be the same:

discouragement, anxiety, and fear. Our problem-solving capacity and confidence will be decreased, and we may suffer physical or emotional illnesses.

Emotion-Focused Financial Stress.

"Never worship any god but me" (Deuteronomy 5:7).
    "You cannot serve two masters: God and money. For you will hate one and love the other, or else the other way around" (Matthew 6:24).
    "You say, 'I am rich, with everything I want; I don't need a thing!' And you don't realize that spiritually you are wretched and miserable and poor and blind and naked" (Revelation 3:17).
    "Gold is a living god," Percy Bysshe Shelley, "Queen Mab."

Each of these statements is a statement about *faith* and about *money*. And each statement implies the fact that emotion-focused financial stress is nothing more than a statement of our trust in God. The higher our level of distress, the lower our level of trust.

When we worry about what might happen to our finances or our security, we place our trust in the finances themselves for security. Emotion-focused financial distress, then, is idolatry. (See Ephesians 5:5.) Faith in money, whether in the form of a retirement plan, investments, property, or the expectation of continuing employment, is not faith in God. It is a direct violation of the First Commandment: "You shall have no other gods before me" (Exodus 20:3, NKJV). And as long as we are in violation of this commandment, we cannot possibly avoid anxiety, apprehension, or fear. So Step One in the managing of emotion-focused financial stress is this: *Establish your faith in the total sovereignty of God.*

Step One: The apostle Paul tells us, "Faith comes from listening to this Good News—the Good News about Christ" (Romans 10:17). In other words, faith is re-established by diligently searching God's Word, where he builds a solid foundation for unshakable and immovable trust in his ability to provide our security.

The prophet Habakkuk anticipated the worst. God was about to destroy the earth, tearing the continents into shreds with flood-engorged rivers, and fracturing the mountains into pieces with the thunder of celestial chariots. The stark terror of inescapable calamity must have clutched at the throat of the prophet. Yet he wrote:

"Even though the fig trees are all destroyed, and there is neither blossom left nor fruit, and though the olive crops all fail, and the fields lie barren; even if the flocks die in the fields and the cattle barns are empty, yet I will rejoice in the Lord; I will be happy in the God of my salvation. The Lord God is my Strength, and he will give me the speed of a deer and bring me safely over the mountains" (Habakkuk 3:17-19).

Clearly, Habakkuk believed that God is the source of our security. He knew that God will always provide everything we need, and that our trust and confidence must be in God.

Less dramatic but equally anxiety-generating circumstances bore down upon the masses who thronged about Jesus during his ministry. His message not only transcended their ritualistic struggles for peace, it dealt with their most fundamental survival needs. He told them:

"You cannot serve two masters: God and money. For you will hate one and love the other, or else the other way around. So my counsel is: Don't worry about things—food,

drink, and clothes. For you already have life and a body—and they are far more important than what to eat and wear. Look at the birds! They don't worry about what to eat—they don't need to sow or reap or store up food—for your heavenly Father feeds them. And you are far more valuable to him than they are. Will all your worries add a single moment to your life?

"So don't worry at all about having enough food and clothing. Why be like the heathen? For they take pride in all these things and are deeply concerned about them. But your heavenly Father already knows perfectly well that you need them, and he will give them to you if you give him first place in your life and live as he wants you to.

"So don't be anxious about tomorrow. God will take care of your tomorrow too. Live one day at a time" (Matthew 6:24-27, 31-34).

The level of trust in God that Christ speaks of cannot coexist with trust in one's own ability to provide for oneself. It is helpful to identify the verses and the historical accounts in the Scriptures which establish this fact. A few of these verses are:

"Always remember that it is the Lord your God who gives you power to become rich" (Deuteronomy 8:18).

"Some he causes to be poor and others to be rich. He cuts one down and lifts another up" (1 Samuel 2:7).

"Everything we have has come from you, and we only give you what is yours already!" (1 Chronicles 29:14).

"The earth belongs to God! Everything in all the world is his" (Psalm 24:1).

"For all the animals of field and forest are mine! The cattle on a thousand hills! And all the birds upon the mountains! . . . for all the world is mine, and everything in it" (Psalm 50:10, 11, 12b).

"The silver is mine, and the gold is mine, says the Lord of hosts" (Haggai 2:8, RSV).

"Don't worry about anything; instead, pray about everything; tell God your needs and don't forget to thank him for his answers. If you do this you will experience God's peace, which is far more wonderful than the human mind can understand. His peace will keep your thoughts and your hearts quiet and at rest as you trust in Christ Jesus" (Philippians 4:6, 7).

"And now just as you trusted Christ to save you, trust him, too, for each day's problems; live in vital union with him" (Colossians 2:6).

Step One has always been the most difficult step in managing financial stress of any kind. But once you've started with this step, the next step is simple.

Step Two: Memorize Scripture. Remember Kennie Anderson's main stress management technique? When he lay awake at night, he repeated—again and again—"What can we ever say to such wonderful things as these? If God is on our side, who can ever be against us?" (Romans 8:31).

Kennie used this Scripture as anxiety welled within him to gain the quieting comfort of God's powerful Word. So the second step in managing financial stress is to find and memorize those Scriptures which communicate God's power and comforting presence. This brings us to Step Three.

Step Three: Apply the Scriptures to your situation. Negative, fear-filled thoughts must be replaced with thoughts that bring a peace "which passes all understanding." Emotion-focused financial stress can be replaced with peace-inducing scriptural promises. Baseball U.S.A.'s Doug Bliss had to cope with both emotion-generated and situation-generated financial stress; but he managed it beautifully. He believed and memorized Scriptures. When the stress grew, he repeated these Scriptures to himself. He accepted God as his security, memorized the scriptural proof of this fact, and constantly applied these Scriptures in his life.

Problem-Focused Stress. Special investigator Samuel Van Pelt, in a study of the economic crisis of farmers in rural Nebraska, reported to the Associated Press in late 1984 his alarm over "seeds of hate" and of a growing "survivalist mentality" in the farm community, resulting in the spread of aggressive and militant publications against Jews and other minority groups. The continuing economic distress of rural America, Van Pelt reported, had caused a breakdown in traditional values.

Most of the people attracted to the "disturbing" literature and to the groups which spawned it "are hard-working, conscientious people who are failing financially." External forces seemed to make a lie of the virtues of honest toil, and diligent stewardship. Fuel prices had run rampant. Grain embargoes had become an instrument of foreign policy. Interest rates soared to unimaginable heights. A 1985 study reported "profound pain and suffering" resulting from stress on farm families. A Nebraska State Patrol SWAT team had to kill a bankrupt farmer who, in desperation, had resorted to armed violence in a frantic attempt to stave off the foreclosure and repossession of his heavily mortgaged farm.

Problem-focused stress differs significantly from emotion-focused stress. Emotion-focused stress, with the right approach, can *always* be avoided. Problem-focused stress, however, can only *sometimes* be avoided, even when we diligently follow guidelines in this area.

Your Life Trust Account: A Stress Insurance Program

Financial stress is so difficult to manage because it is always concerned, ultimately, with the problem of basic survival. Yet, there are ways to protect oneself against financial distress which do not require money. Pastor

Harry Spykerman, a South African minister, was once responsible for acquiring and administering funds in a "faith" ministry that affected fifty-five missionary families on the African continent. He developed the idea of the Life Trust Account, containing scripturally-derived principles in a step-by-step financial stress management program. If followed, this program can help one to encounter stress without incurring distress, and it can result in developing a new perspective on such encounters. This Life Trust Account Insurance Program follows:

Step One: Write, in full, each of the Scripture verses listed below. These verses declare that God has given you everything. (No successful program for stress management of financial problems is possible without acceptance of the fact embraced in this first step!)

> *Luke 12:6, 7*
> *Acts 17:25, 28*
> *Romans 8:31*
> *Romans 12:6*
> *Philippians 2:13*
> *Philippians 4:19*
> *Colossians 1:7*
> *1 Timothy 1:12*
> *1 Timothy 2:13*
> *Hebrews 10:38*
> *1 Peter 5:6, 7*
> *1 John 5:14, 15*

Step Two: Confirm your total dependence upon God by tithing what he has given to you. No, tithing is not a divine New Testament mandate. And no, tithing is not, as "health and wealth" theology teaches, a magic formula that guarantees a tangible material return on the dollar. Tithing, in Harry Spykerman's program, is an insurance policy against financial distress. Notice that the insurance policy protects you against distress, not stress. But if and when financial stress is encountered, Rev. Spykerman asserts, it can be faced without anxiety.

When you tithe, you acknowledge God as Provider. (See Deuteronomy 14:21, 23.) Each time you tithe, you reaffirm the belief that God provides your finances. In essence, tithing is an overt act of the will that reinforces and solidifies the conviction that it is God who *has* provided, it is God who *now* provides, and it is God who *will continue* to provide. This conviction builds up a store of inner resources of obedience and trust. And it is these resources that you will be able to draw upon when faced with even the most dire of financial problems.

Step Three: List all of your assets for which God has given you at least some decision-making power. That is, what do you have that can be shared, used, or given by you to serve Jesus Christ or other people?

Step Four: Determine for yourself that your chief task is to be a caretaker or a steward of what God has given you. You are, in Rev. Spykerman's terminology, a "Life Trust Account," into which God makes deposits and from which you make withdrawals. In this sense, each of us serves as God's channel for distributing his wealth. And God's wealth, as it relates to economic security, is made up of your job, your time, your abilities, your resources—your total being!

One fact about stress now becomes obvious: You cannot suffer the distress of envy, jealousy, or covetousness when you recognize the source and understand the nature of your resources—including money—and accept the purpose for which you were given those resources. And you will be able to manage more successfully the stress of inadequate finances if you remember that it is *your* job to do your best for God with your time, abilities, and resources, and it is *God's* job to do his best for you by providing you with opportunities and income. No opportunity or income exists that doesn't come from God.

Step Five: Make a written commitment. This is an extremely difficult step to take, because as Rev. Spykerman stated:

"This is the offering up of a whole life to the Lord Jesus. It means offering yourself as a living sacrifice. This goes against the grain of an unenlightened person, who still considers that what he has belongs to him, and that the Lord has become a convenient help in improving his position and prospering himself. So what he shares with the Lord and others is his own prerogative and depends on how generous and accommodating he feels.

"His benefactory generosity makes him proud, believing that out of 'goodness of heart' he is sacrificing his things to the Lord."

Now, if Steps One to Four have made you ready for Step Five, then you can make your written commitment by filling in the blanks below:

Life Trust Account Contract.

I, _____, unequivocally believe that everything I have comes from God alone. I believe that God has given me resources that I can share with others. I will overtly acknowledge God as my total source of security by deciding to give to him _____ percent of my total income, regardless of my financial condition, to reinforce and strengthen my faith that God alone provides me with everything. When faced with financial stress, I shall restudy each of the Scriptures listed in the preceding pages, I shall reread this contract, and I shall again note that I have signed and dated my written statement of total dependence upon God.

(Signed) _____

(Date) _____

Step Six: Review Steps One through Five periodically. This helps you reinforce them, and, according to Rev. Spykerman, "That which is reinforced is strengthened."

Avoiding Financial Stress

The Spykerman model is a realistic, scripturally substantiable approach for both managing *and* avoiding financial stress. However, although we can deal with distress, we must still face disruptions in economic stability, ranging from the monumental (such as the Great Depression) to the mundane (such as a blown head gasket in an automobile). The Bible is full of guidelines for avoiding some financial problems. Some of the guidelines are *im*plicit—they lead to inferences that can be logically drawn, and that prove in practice to be both feasible and defensible. Other guidelines are clearly *ex*plicit—God directly tells us what to do.

The "Foolishness" of God's Approach. Almost everybody enjoys the unusual, the novel, the inexplicable. For years, "Believe It or Not," an illustrated column by George Ripley, entertained millions of newspaper readers, stretching their credulity and defying their logic. Soon, several imitators created equally intriguing curiosities under similiar titles; "Strange, but True," another illustrated column, paralleled the tantalizing trivia of Ripley's newspaper accounts; TV's "That's Incredible!" competed for viewer loyalty with televised versions of "Believe It or Not" and "The Guinness Book of World Records." Whatever the name, though, the content was the same. Truth, in many instances, was indeed shown to be stranger than fiction.

And any of these phrases—"believe it or not," "that's incredible," and "strange, but true"—could be applied to some of the scriptural precepts about the managing of finances. Often, God's instructions appear to make absolutely no sense in the real world. But they are undeniably valid, and if they are followed, they can help us avoid the anxiety and distress of financial matters.

For example, the following strategies of financial management probably would not be advocated by even one professional financial planning service or investment counselor:

1. Even though community consciousness and participation in charitable endeavor can enhance your personal and professional status and result in increased business, and other personal and professional benefits, do not seek accolades from the community. Instead, strive to remain totally unrecognized for your generosity. (See Matthew 6:1-4.)

2. Certain agencies and individuals will seek to obtain unsecured loans from you, offering no collateral. In fact, in some cases, the loan, in Shakespeare's words, will "lose both itself and friend." Nevertheless, loan these people the money. Loan it even if they seek to ruin you or your business, and don't concern yourself with the repayment probability. (See Proverbs 20; Matthew 5:43; Luke 6:34, 35; 2 Thessalonians 3:10; and James 2:16.)

3. If others are convinced that they are entitled to have what is rightly yours, and they overtly and aggressively demand it of you, give it to them. And don't concern yourself with ways to get it

back. (See Matthew 5:40, 41; Luke 6:29, 30;
1 Corinthians 6:7; and Hebrews 11:34.)

4. Make what is yours available to others for their use. (See Hebrews 6:11; 13:2-4; and 1 Peter 4:9.)

5. When with people from varying economic levels, don't show any differentiation. Don't concern yourself with professional contacts or potentially profitable business associations. (See Proverbs 23:1; 28:1, 21; and James 2:1-9.)

6. If you have the basic necessities, don't concern yourself with cash flow, liquidity, or investment plans. Give most of your money away; use it to benefit both friends and strangers. (See 1 Timothy 6:6-10.)

7. Give your work and business the attention it deserves; but if it starts interfering with your relationships, pull back. Don't get preoccupied with business transactions. (See Proverbs 23:4, 5; Colossians 3:2; and 2 Timothy 2:4.)

8. Make a genuine effort to share everything you have. If you are really generous, you won't have enough money left over to be considered affluent. And that is when you'll become truly rich. (See Proverbs 11:24-26; and 13:7.)

This financial advice seems to stretch credulity and flout rationality. It is contrary to every rule of contemporary business practice. It seems the opposite of good, solid, "prudent" business advice. But what has good solid, prudent business advice produced? Often its results are anger, strife, frustration, turmoil, and distress.

Following man's "conventional financial wisdom" calls for asserting and promoting your self-interests. Yet, whether you win or lose your financial conflicts following this advice, you will inevitably lose in the areas of peace of mind, health, and tranquility of spirit.

When your only concern is to assert your self-interest, loss and distress are the results.

There is an enormous emotional price when we strive to be recognized for all the good we do for others, and no one notices us. We brood over our "wasted" time, grow resentful and angry, and often resort to boasting to be noticed. And then, when it's our boasting that is noticed, we lose again.

Self-interest tells us to concoct excuses, construct elaborate facades, or even lie to avoid "friends" seeking a loan or an outright handout. Our excuses, facades, lies, and deceit cost emotional energy, and soon sap us of serenity and inner peace.

Peace of mind, a patient disposition, and other personal riches from God are also lost when we relentlessly pursue repayment of overdue loans. We pit our time, emotions, and energy against people whose creativity in avoiding repayment is often exceeded only by their dishonesty and selfishness. We destroy our very spirit and our health, in the mental turmoil of devising schemes and strategies for recapturing what has been taken from us. Then we degrade ourselves when our efforts fail and we are forced to choke down the bile of defeat and frustration.

An assertion of self-interest for material gain at the expense of others drains any spiritual serenity we may have. The application of conventional wisdom finds us thirsting for peace of mind, standing, in utter distress, with our reservoir of spiritual refreshment totally depleted. God's formula and wisdom, on the other hand, have some very different perspectives and results. He calls us to yield our self-interest, and to gain his blessings. When our primary concern is our spiritual welfare, and the spiritual welfare of our brothers and sisters, the only thing we will lose is our bondage to distress!

Compare the two financial formulas—man's and

God's—side by side. Which do you believe will be best for managing the stress of conflicts and disputes in financial matters?

PLAN "A"
God's Formula
Yield self-interest, lose conflict=Win God's blessings.

Yield self-interest, win conflict=Win God's blessings, as well as the dispute.

Lose=Win
Win=Win
Final Outcome: Win

"My son, never forget the things I've taught you. If you want a long and satisfying life, closely follow my instructions" (Proverbs 3:1, 2).

PLAN "B"
Man's Formula
Assert self-interest, but lose conflict=Lose piece of mind and spiritual tranquility.

Assert self-interest, and win conflict=Lose peace of mind, etc.

Lose=Lose
Win=Lose
Final Outcome: Lose

"There is a way that seemeth right unto a man, but the end thereof are the ways of death" (Proverbs 16:25, KJV).

But What about My Rights? Plan A or Plan B? The first is both revolutionary, and two thousand years old! But the way of YAHWEH has been pushed aside time after time, for the way of YABWIF ("Yes, But What If . . .").

"Good master," we mouth, in imitation of the insincere flatterer whose insincerity Jesus denounced in Matthew 19, and then we proceed to construct a hypothetical barrier to make the direct teaching of Jesus Christ seem absurd.

*"And if someone demands your coat, give him your shirt
besides." "Yes, but what if it's a Russian sable coat
purchased as an investment which is later to be donated to
a fund to compensate unemployed residents of Labrador
who lost their livelihood because of government prohibition
of the killing of baby seals . . . and what if . . ."*

And on we go, blinded to God's goodness by our
"rights" and "logic." But the only rights we can assert
are those given to us by Christ. Our scriptural criterion
for action brings us again to the principle discussed in
Chapter 4, that we have a major purpose in life.
Assertion of our "rights" in disputes over finances is
governed by the fact that our major purpose in life is
that of being living examples of the love of Jesus
Christ. We serve others to help them attain their
ultimate salvation.

Conventional wisdom cannot serve this purpose.
When we wrestle and struggle with others, brawling
over or hoarding material possessions, we destroy the
message of Christ's Gospel. We become no different
than the world. We have, like Esau, "sold our birthright
for a mess of pottage" (Genesis 20:29-33). We have *no*
right to assert our self-interest to the extent that we
prevent others from experiencing Christ's love through
us.

Plan A—God's plan of unconventional wisdom, or
Plan B—man's plan of conventional wisdom? Plan A
and *freedom from* distress, or Plan B and *domination by*
distress? Which will it be? For the Christian, the answer
is obvious: There is no Plan B. But while the choice is
clear, the method of implementation is not.

Tips on Trading: Avoiding Financial Problems
Bill and Dave seemed to be ideal partners. Although
they held widely divergent religious beliefs (Dave

was a Christian, Bill was not), they both knew the construction business. They had similar work habits, and both took pride in their ability to succeed. They agreed to build a house. It would be a three bedroom ranch-style home in red brick, with three baths and two fireplaces. Dave would use his own home as collateral.

The profits would be satisfying—the last home Bill had built had turned a healthy 40 percent net in 1971, even with concrete costing twenty-four dollars a yard. He had done some quick mental calculation, figuring one hundred and fifty days to completion. The quotes on plumbing, carpeting, excavating, backfilling, and appliances were still out, but he had a rough idea of what it all would take.

The realtor had told him the area was growing, and that the three main elements in moving a property were "location, location, and location." The bentonite soil base, which only sometimes shifted and caused foundations to crack, had not been noticed by Dave or Bill and would not be noticed by a potential buyer.

Construction began, then slowed. The pollen was bad and Bill's hay fever was uncomfortable. Then, too, it was chilly in the cool spring mornings. Warmer days lay ahead, and full days and weeks of work could be put in later. When the work finally started in earnest, the pace was so frantic that the dirt which formed the base for the concrete wasn't water-settled. But then the pace slackened again. Deadlines were missed, bookkeeping was sloppy, bills piled up and carrying charges climbed to 21 percent.

Incredibly, Dave had neglected to tell Bill that he had planned for electric heat, while Bill had planned for forced air. Bill was doing the back of the house in used, red brick—rustic and antique—in a Roman bond pattern. Dave, meanwhile, was hauling new red brick, anticipating its crisp look. The fireplaces failed to pass inspection—inadequate footings. Bill had planned fireboxes. Dave, ignorant of fireboxes, had contracted for masonry work. But the cost of concrete at ninety dollars a yard had not even been imagined. Debts mounted, interest piled upon interest, liens were filed . . . and sharp words were exchanged.

Bill initiated litigation against Dave, defaulted on the loan, and dropped the project. Dave, the cosigner, watched the foreclosure on his pledged home with dismay. The housing development promised by the realtor did not materialize. No city water would be available, and well permits were unobtainable. There were no savings set aside to draw from to carry either Bill or Dave through their financial calamity. Now the disaster was complete.

Perhaps the greatest tragedy for these two men was not the fact of their financial collapse. Rather it was the fact that every stress they experienced could have been avoided, had they been guided by Scripture.

Both their problems and the Scriptures which offered them guidance were many:

Problem	Scripture Helps
1. The partners were well-matched in every characteristic except for the most fundamental characteristic: Their spiritual faith. They did not have a common basis for conflict resolution or stress reduction.	*2 Corinthians 6:14*
2. Closely related to the first problem is the fact that they could not jointly "commit their work unto the Lord."	*Proverbs 16:3* *Psalm 127:1*
3. Careful financial accounting did not take place. Instead of making a careful, meticulous cost estimation, an ill-advised "rough guess"	*Proverbs 14:8; 15:22* *Luke 14: 28-33*

Problem	**Scripture Helps**
constituted the basis for financial commitments.	
4. Hasty speculation and the desire to turn a quick profit led to a lack of communication on basics, such as heating, masonry work, and other vital elements.	*Proverbs 21:5; 22:3; 27:12; 28:22; 23-27*
5. Inadequate counsel on the location, and an incredible naivete—believing the word of one real estate representative—led to great adversity when the construction site was found to be isolated.	*Proverbs 13:11; 14:5, 15; 15:22; 28:22*
6. Sloppy bookkeeping and tardiness in making payments resulted in punitive interest charges and ultimate foreclosure.	*Proverbs 3:27; 22:7*
7. Work did not proceed with diligence. Excuses to procrastinate and to avoid task orientation and commitment were found.	*Proverbs 6:6; 10:5; 14:23; 20:4, 13; 21:17, 25, 26; 22:13; 24:31; 26:13; 28:19 Ecclesiastes 9:10*
8. Neither man kept abreast of the facts. Concrete had gone from twenty-four dollars to ninety dollars. Fireboxes had largely replaced total masonry work, sometimes even in custom homes.	*Proverbs 24:3, 4*

Problem	**Scripture Helps**
9. The attempt to conceal potential structural defects (bentonite soil) and to take shortcuts (pouring concrete over unsettled backfill), was dishonest, and would have caused subsequent problems.	*Proverbs 16:1; 19:1; 20:10*
10. Dave lacked adequate resources to cosign on a loan. In essence, he pledged his very bed as collateral.	*Proverbs 6:1-5; 11:15; 17:18; 22:26, 27*
11. Both partners failed to hold any finances in reserve for possible future adversity.	*Proverbs 21:20; 30:24-28*

Other advice for financial stress avoidance includes advice to pay taxes gladly (Romans 13:6, 7), to pay God first (Proverbs 3:9, 10), to share generously with others (Proverbs 19:17; 27:10; 28:27), and to avoid striving to build a fortune (Proverbs 28:23-27; Matthew 6:19-20) while at the same time providing for dependents (Proverbs 13:22; 21:20; 27:12). The Scriptures provide additional counsel about incurring debt (Romans 13:8) and avoiding the debasing practice of currying the favor of affluent people (Proverbs 23:1; James 2:1). The benefits of making the most of opportunity (Proverbs 10:5; 12:9), and making the best use of time (Ecclesiastes 11:4) are also extolled.

Summary
Every potential source of financial distress, whether emotion- or problem-focused, is identified in the Scriptures. God has provided us with specific steps to avoid financial distress when possible, and to manage

the financial stress that's unavoidable. Unlike the most secure of financial investments, the divinely-inspired, scriptural steps to avoiding and managing financial stress offer a 100 percent guarantee of success.

Eight
Is It All in Your Head?
Stress and the Mind/Body Connection

What's the Connection?

Each of us can be certain that troubles will come into our lives. The way we handle these troubles determines how stress will affect us. Often, mismanaged stress is manifested in a physical way, causing pain or disease. However, this type of distress response can be avoided.

When the ancient Hebrews left Egypt under the leadership of Moses, God made them a promise: "I will not make you suffer the diseases I sent on the Egyptians, for I am the Lord who heals you" (Exodus 15:26). There were many Egyptian illnesses that the Jews feared, such as blindness from venereal disease, leg ulcers, consumption, and a condition called *elephantiasis* which caused massive swelling of the legs. God promised to keep the Hebrews free from such diseases, but only if certain conditions were met. The Hebrews were required to: listen carefully to the voice of the Lord, do what is right, pay attention to God's commands, and keep all of God's decrees.

And it's very much the same today—when we live apart from God's directions and decrees, distress will result. Personal problems and numerous illnesses may develop because of our separation from God.

In the Doctor's Office. Karen Haines is a retired schoolteacher in her seventies who complained bitterly of pain, muscle cramps, and burning in her neck, arms, and shoulders. Her symptoms had been present for years, and she had been to many doctors, including experts in well-known medical centers. Now she eyed her doctor warily as she once again described her symptoms, taking his hand and placing it on a tender spot on her neck to show it more clearly. She was putting him to the test, to find out if he could "doctor" her.

He reviewed her medical records as they talked, finding that numerous tests had already been done. The results were all normal. While the doctor stared at the papers in front of him, Karen sat with her arms folded across her chest. Methodically, laboriously, he began his examination, thinking of what other doctors had told her: "psychosomatic." The word rang over and over in his mind. It seemed to be the only logical explanation. However, she insistently rejected this explanation, with bitter observations about the "professionalism" of the doctors who had told her the pain was all in her head. If she were to be helped, the doctor decided, he must use a different approach—a creative one. Finishing the examination, an intuition born of many years of experience prompted him to question her about more personal matters.

"Do you live alone?" he asked

Her response was immediate—eager, almost. "My husband died twelve years ago. I've been alone ever since." Her wrist brushed against her eyes in a poorly concealed attempt to hide her tears.

"Do you have family nearby?" he asked.

"No," she replied. "I have two sons, but they live on the East Coast, and I haven't seen them for years."

"Then you're all alone."

"Yes," she said, with a faint, defiant smile on her face. He paused reflectively.

"Hmm," he said. "What do you do with your free time?"

Her response was defensive. "Don't worry yourself about that!" she blurted. "I have many projects to keep me busy. Lately I have been remodeling my kitchen."

He ignored her tone and pressed forward. "Do you have grandchildren?"

"Yes, three."

"Do you ever see them?"

"I haven't for a long time, several years." Again she grew defiant. "But that doesn't bother me. I'm used to it."

He explained that nothing concrete could be found to explain her pains, and a knowing smile emerged on her lips. So this new doctor was joining all the others who were unable to find a cause for her ailments. Still searching for a way to help her, he made a suggestion.

"Why don't you visit your children? And your grandchildren?"

She mused pensively for a moment. Then she replied, "Do you really think I ought to? I've been thinking about it. But since my husband died, I've stayed away."

"It might do you some good," he said encouragingly.

Karen did indeed visit her family, and it was a joyous reunion for all. And soon, though she received no medication or treatment, her malady disappeared—for good!

Many people like this retired teacher enter doctors' offices complaining of physical ailments. But their suffering is in their emotions, thoughts, and feelings. They are unaware of the link between the mind and the body.

These tense, anxious people have stress-related

illnesses such as headaches, depression, alcoholism, obesity, hypertension, and intestinal problems. Often, they are heavy smokers. It is estimated that more than 70 percent of the people who go to doctors today are suffering from psychosomatic illnesses. These illnesses stem from an unspoken, inner pain, caused by such situations as the loss of a loved one, a job problem, financial difficulties, troubles with children, or worry about serious illness such as cancer. When these people are told that nothing seems to be wrong, they usually react with anger and dismay. They see the doctor as unfriendly and uncaring. Often such a patient will feel rejected, which adds to his distress in perceiving himself as a person who, he is sure, is regarded by his doctor as a hypochondriac, even though he "knows" he is sick.

In the Hospital. It was two A.M. when the phone rang and the doctor wearily placed the receiver by his ear, fighting off the urge to go back to sleep. A familiar voice pierced the silence of the night.

"Dr. Jones, this is Dr. Williams. I have a young lady in the emergency room who is having uncontrolled epileptic seizures. So far she's been given dilantin, valium, and phenobarbital, with no success. I need help."

Dr. Jones' response was immediate and concerned. "Admit her to the ward," he directed, "and I'll be there shortly."

When the doctor arrived, the ward was electrified with commotion. The nursing supervisor was the first to greet him.

"Good morning, Dr. Jones," she said.

"What's going on?" he replied, unconsciously ignoring her practiced formality.

"The new patient, Mrs. Fare, is having another seizure. We tried calling you, but your wife said you had already left." An uneasy feeling aroused him to greater alertness as the nurse continued. "Mrs. Fare's seizures worsened the moment she arrived on the ward." Together they went into the room where the young woman lay. A tongue blade was jammed between her teeth, her arms and legs were jerking, and she moaned.

"Start intravenous medication right away," Dr. Jones instructed.

As the anti-seizure drug was injected, the twitching, convulsive movements ceased, and the woman was still. When she regained consciousness, she began sobbing quietly, then lapsed into sleep.

"With all this medication she won't have another seizure tonight," Dr. Jones told the nurse. "Call me if you have any problems."

He looked at his watch as he went to his car. It was 4:15 A.M. There would be enough time for a couple of hours of sleep before beginning another busy day. Soon he was settled comfortably beneath the covers and sound asleep. The jangling of the phone jarred him back into wakefulness.

"Dr. Jones, this is the nurse calling about Mrs. Fare. She's having another seizure."

"I don't believe it!" he exclaimed. "After all that medication?"

"I'm afraid so, Doctor."

"Give her another injection and move her to intensive care. If her seizure doesn't stop, call me right back." He was now awake, pondering for a few minutes the unusual nature of the case. The phone rang again. It was the nurse.

"Doctor, we gave her the medication as you ordered."

"Good," he replied impatiently, "did it stop the seizure?"

"Yes, it worked well, the patient is awake and talking. Now we have a new problem. I don't know how to say this. Here, let me put the nursing supervisor on the phone." There was a moment of silence, and by now his curiosity was heightened.

"This is Miss Jantz, Nursing Supervisor."

"Miss Jantz, just what is going on?'

"Your new patient, the one with the seizures . . ."

"Yes, go on, is something wrong?" he asked, fearing the worst.

"Yes, Mrs. Fare refuses to go to intensive care. We've all talked to her. Her family has talked with her. It's no use, she won't cooperate."

"Miss Jantz, who is running the hospital, you or the patient? Carry out your orders right away."

"Yes, Doctor," she replied. As he hung up, Dr. Jones shook his head. In a few minutes the phone rang again. It was a nurse from intensive care.

"Doctor, your patient, Mrs. Fare, is having another seizure."

"I'll be there right away."

When he arrived at the woman's bedside, he studied her seizure carefully and noticed that it was unusual, not like any he had seen before. When he tried to examine the patient, she raised her arm to push him away, screamed, arched her back, and began to sob as her body jerked convulsively. And then he knew.

"This is not epilepsy," he thought. "This is an emotional seizure." Testing his less-than-tentative conjecture, he diligently observed the patient until there was no room for doubt. He was now sure: The problem stemmed from the patient's emotions.

Several hours later he obtained the woman's history from her family. Helen Fare had been having such seizures since childhood. They came on if she was frustrated or upset about something. The onset of this attack was no different. Her husband had announced the night before that he wanted a divorce. Almost immediately, her seizures began.

Dr. Jones had discovered the real problem, and prescribed a visit with a counselor. After several counseling sessions, Mrs. Fare suffered no further seizures, and she was able to return home.

The Real Problem

Helen Fare entered the hospital with what seemed to be a serious, even life-threatening medical problem. Many patients convince their families and doctors that they are seriously ill with heart attacks, gall bladder problems, severe pain, convulsive seizures—but they're all responding to a major life crisis. Because the patient and doctor focus on the physical problem at hand, their search for answers is futile. Only 2 percent of patients tell their doctors about their personal problems, because they see no connection between their physical suffering and their personal anguish.

For some people, illness is a way of life. They wander from doctor to doctor in search of an answer to their health problems. They have many symptoms, but no disease. Common experiences of these people include divorce, self-neglect, alcoholism, loss of self-esteem, or the recent death of a family member. Many of the people have had physical problems for months. But it's a crisis in their personal life, not a physical illness, that is causing the problem.

So, there are three reasons why people enter the hospital: (1) They are sick; (2) they have malfunctioning bodies usually caused by inappropriate responses to stress; or (3) they have disturbed interpersonal or social relationships. For more than 40 percent of those people entering hospitals today, stress is the underlying cause of the illness.

How the Mind-Body Link Works. For stress to cause disease, the mind must somehow affect the body. Medical scientists have studied this problem since the turn of the century. Dr. Walter Cannon discovered the "fight or flight reaction." If an animal or a person is confronted with a sudden threatening situation, a physiological reaction occurs. The heart beats faster, blood pressure rises, and muscles tense, preparing the individual to either fight or to run away. When the danger is past, the functions return to normal with no adverse effects. The experience was a brief, but intense, reaction to danger which caused chemical changes in the body.

In the 1930s Dr. Hans Selye, a pioneer in the analysis of stress, made some startling discoveries. He took blood serum from an animal which had been angered, and injected it into another animal, a rabbit. The rabbit died almost immediately! The offending chemical was adrenaline, produced by the adrenal gland. The conclusion was as obvious as it was definite: The effects of stress can be adverse, even dangerous.

Dr. Selye made numerous discoveries about chronic stress. For example, the source of stress varies considerably. What is stressful to one person might not be so stressful to another. Finally, Selye discovered that an animal subjected to stress for an extended period of time either adapted to the situation, or it died. So, he concluded, stress—or distress—can kill.

When you are under chronic stress, complex reactions occur in your brain. The hypothalamus, a small area near the pituitary gland in the center of the brain, undergoes numerous chemical changes. Given enough stress over a prolonged period of time, such diseases as high blood pressure, ulcers, headaches, or skin disease may occur.

Another Source of Stress. A young couple sat next to one another, watching in astonishment at what was happening before their eyes. Each one had a feeling of intense horror and fear. He reached for her hand to comfort and reassure her, and she held on tightly. As they watched the danger before them, sweat appeared on their brows, their hearts were racing, their blood pressure increased, hormones were released from their adrenal glands, and their intestinal motility quieted. Suddenly, in a moment of silence, she whimpered in fear. Within a few minutes, the fear was replaced by an ecstasy of happiness, love, and contentment, with music in the background.

The couple was sitting in a movie theater, and nothing was really happening except that they were watching a series of images projected onto a screen. Yet their bodies had reacted as if the event they watched was real. They felt intense anger, fear, and horror, and then love, ecstasy, and freedom. What we see and experience *does* affect our body functions. It does not even have to be real. The inner screen of our imagination causes reactions just as intense as if the situation was real.

When someone drives too close, honks his horn, and shakes his fist, cursing all the while, most of us become angered. As he drives away, we continue to react, imagining the situation over and over, often until it ruins our day. We also imagine wreaking revenge upon the one who offended us, experiencing all the emotions that would create. Through our imaginations, daily hassles lived over and over again become stress inducers. So our response to a situation makes it distressful, if we let it.

Abraham Lincoln said, "A man is as happy as he makes up his mind to be." Our reactions often determine the effect a stressor will have upon us, not the nature of the stressor itself.

A Woman Healed. A large crowd numbering in the thousands milled about, waiting for a famous man who was about to pass by. In the masses stood a woman, brooding silently about her misery. For years she had had an incurable problem with uncontrollable bleeding. She had found no cure or help from any of the numerous doctors she had visited. She had spent all her life savings, to no avail. Still, she had not given up hope that someday she would be cured. That's why she was there among all the others. She had heard of this man, Jesus. Perhaps he could help her. She watched as he approached, standing tall among his disciples who gently pushed a path for him through the crowd. Many people just wanted to touch him. The woman found herself thrust forward by the crowds, and she reached out and grasped the hem of his robe. In her heart she prayed she would be healed of her illness . . . and she was! The issue of blood had stopped!

Suddenly Jesus stopped.

"Who touched me?" he exclaimed. His disciples hesitated in confusion.

"Master, there are so many here," one of them answered. "How can we know who you are seeking, for many have touched you."

"Power has gone out of me. Find out who the person is, so I can talk with him."

Slowly the woman rose from her knees, for she was in prayer, thanking God for healing her. She went forward to Jesus.

"Lord, I am the one you seek," she said tearfully. "I touched your hem when you walked by."

Jesus looked down at her, and gently held his hand out to her.

"Woman, why have you done this thing?" he asked.

"For years I have suffered from an issue of blood. When you walked by, I knew in my heart I would be healed if only I could reach out and touch you."

Jesus smiled warmly, "It was your faith which healed you. Go in peace, for you are now free."

In this account from Mark 5:25-34, Jesus bridged the invisible barrier between mind and body. We are not told by the writers of the New Testament of the troubles this woman had experienced. This fact is not important. What we are told is that she was healed because of a change in her spirit, and the effect on the healing of her body was immediate and complete—it was accomplished by faith. There is a gap between the body, the spirit, and mind, that can only be bridged by Jesus Christ, the greatest healer who ever lived.

Summary

When we live apart from the decrees of God, we will respond inappropriately to stress. This mismanagement of stress, or distress, often results in physical changes and illnesses. It has been discovered that many patients who go to see doctors or who are in the hospital are suffering from illnesses related to or caused by distress.

But the Christian can avoid this result of distress by realizing that Jesus, our great physician, can reach through the Spirit to heal our bodies. He can guide us to appropriate responses to stress, and to better mental and physical health.

Nine
Chronic Stress and Illness

"That Makes Me Sick!"

While acute stressful situations can produce immediate responses, such as the "fight or flight" reaction, chronic distress can lead to chemical and hormonal changes in the body. These changes can make one susceptible to real physical illness.

When someone becomes sick, there are usually several forces involved: natural (medical) causes; inappropriate responses to stress; and spiritual problems.

Most illnesses are determined by natural phenomena in the environment. For instance, infections occur from viruses or bacteria. Some examples of illnesses resulting from natural or medical causes include:

Ulcers—due to erosion of the lining of the stomach caused by acid.

Heart attacks—from clogging of the coronary arteries with cholesterol.

Skin rashes—psoriasis, neurodermatitis, aggravated by stress.

Strokes—blockage of brain arteries by cholesterol.

Colitis—inflammation of the lining of the colon.

Cancer—unrestrained growth of malignant cells.

Any of these types of illnesses can be "triggered" by stressful situations, or a weakened physical condition. One of the most common "triggers" for illness is physical exhaustion. Someone who spends long hours at work may be a prime candidate for pneumonia. Arduous work and long hours, with insufficient rest, constitute an inappropriate response to the stress of a demanding task-oriented personality. The "natural" cause of an onset of illness is a bacterial infection. Job stress and fatigue, however, were the "trigger events." Whether the "triggers" shoot a bullet or a blank depends on our response.

Research in psychosomatic medicine has found that people often have a "weak link," a part of the body prone to develop illness when under stress. The susceptible target organ for the person with asthma is the lungs. A sudden crisis such as a family argument, financial problems, or trouble with one's children may precipitate a severe attack of wheezing and "air hunger." The breathing passageways contract, and congestion builds in the lungs, making it difficult for the person to breathe. Should the attack become severe, panic can occur, which only worsens the attack. Thus a cycle of stress and real illness is created.

A Lesson from Elijah. The prophet Elijah had reached a point of despair after his confrontation with King Ahab, as recorded in the Old Testament in 1 Kings. Ahab reigned over Israel, the northern kingdom of Palestine, an area notorious for its godless ways and worship of idols. After three years of drought, the land and the people were desperate and turned to their pagan gods for help. So Elijah challenged the prophets of Baal at Mount Carmel.

At exactly the time for the usual evening sacrifice, Elijah called down fire from heaven and defeated the four hundred and fifty prophets of Baal. Then he killed all of them. Next he prayed for rain to come to the parched land. When the clouds gathered over the Mediterranean Sea, Elijah ran to Jezreel on foot, a distance of more than twenty miles, to announce the coming storm. He even outran the horses drawing the chariot of King Ahab.

When Queen Jezebel heard that Elijah had killed Baal's prophets, she was furious and threatened to kill him within the day. Afraid of Queen Jezebel and her threats, Elijah fled for his life, into the Judean wilderness. He finally collapsed with exhaustion. That night he prayed, "I have had enough! Take away my life."

While he slept, an angel appeared and ordered Elijah to eat. This gave him strength to travel yet another forty days and nights to Mount Horeb. But when he arrived he felt sorry for himself. He cried out to God, saying he was the only one left in Israel who had not broken God's covenants, and now his enemies were after him. Finally, the Lord intervened and gave Elijah further directions for his purpose in life. He gently reminded Elijah that there were seven thousand others in Israel who had not broken his covenants. (See 1 Kings 18:16–19:21.)

Elijah was setting himself up for sickness. He was depressed and physically exhausted by the time he arrived in the wilderness. But God intervened and commanded him to eat, to spend time in prayer, and to listen for his voice. And when Elijah eventually returned to Israel, he witnessed the destruction of King Ahab and Queen Jezebel, his former enemies.

When we arrive in our own "wilderness" of despair and exhaustion, our resistance to disease is at its lowest point. Elijah's experience shows us how to renew our strength through prayer and obedience to the Lord. This is the Lord's creative alternative to sickness.

Ulcers. Dr. Bill Turner is a forty-five-year-old surgeon who is an absolute terror in the operating room. If an instrument is not placed in his hand at exactly the right moment, he's known to explode in a rage. He is a critical person who is intolerant of any human error, no matter how small. Throughout his career, he drove himself as hard as he drove everyone else, mercilessly demanding perfection every moment. To make matters worse, he was hated by almost everyone who worked with him. Few people admired his quest for perfection or saw it as the mark of a good surgeon.

As the years passed, his behavior seemed to get worse, until some of the nurses refused to assist him with surgery. His browbeating and critical attitude had demoralized them. His surgical colleagues urged him to calm down and be more tolerant of others. They all acknowledged he was a good surgeon, one of the best. He listened quietly, nodding assent at the friendly concern shown to him, but his behavior didn't change.

One morning during a difficult surgical procedure, he felt a gnawing pain in the midsection of his stomach. He attributed it to too much coffee. But the pain kept coming back and waves of nausea broke his concentration. Sweat poured from his brow, and others noticed that something was wrong. His assistant surgeon asked if he felt well, but Bill ignored him and requested another instrument from the nurse. Suddenly, without warning, he fell to his knees and began to vomit blood. The pain in his abdomen became excruciating. Within moments he was unconscious, and was rushed to the emergency ward, while his assistant completed the operation.

After he regained consciousness, Bill saw numerous tubes in his arms and a large tube in his nose. Several units of blood were running simultaneously into his veins, replacing what he had vomited. Then a familiar voice spoke. It was Dr. Cliff Sorrel, a colleague and friend.

"Bill, we've found an ulcer. You have serious bleeding and you need surgery right away."

"Are you sure?" asked Bill in dismay.

"There's no question about it. You've lost over twelve units of blood, and it comes out as fast as we put it in. It's a miracle you're still alive. We have a good chance to stop the bleeding if we act right away. Your blood pressure is stable, at least for the moment. Fortunately, you have a good, strong heart. We must operate as soon as possible."

Bill hated hasty decisions, but he knew his friend was right. The pain and nausea were returning, as the bleeding started again.

"Go ahead with the operation, Cliff. If I weren't so sick, I'd insist on being your assistant."

Cliff laughed at Bill's attempt at maintaining a cheerful front. "Some other time. You're in no shape for this one."

Within minutes Bill was unconscious, thanks to the skillful anesthesiologist, and mercifully relieved of pain. As he had lost consciousness, he had looked up to see a nurse, and recognized her as one he had criticized on many different occasions. She disliked him intensely, and for a moment he tried to speak, to say he was sorry, but it was too late. The operation was already beginning.

Later, when he awoke in his room, he saw Cliff standing, holding a specimen jar containing the ulcer. Bill peered closely at the stomach tissue—his tissue. In the center was a deep, craggy ulcer, and in the middle was a blood vessel eaten through by stomach acid. He noticed the pain and nausea were gone.

"Here's the culprit," Cliff said quietly. "I've never seen a worse looking ulcer. You would have died without surgery."

"You're right, Cliff," said Bill. "It had to come out. Thanks."

Cliff smiled, relieved that the ordeal was over, and spoke as he touched Bill's shoulder.

"I'll see you in the morning."

The real problem for Dr. Bill was not the ulcer, but his life-style. He was a perfectionist—intolerant, arrogant, and pompous—but an excellent surgeon. Years of encountering too many frustrations finally took their toll. Unless this man changed his behavior, it would only be a matter of time until some other illness set in.

Heart Disease. In their book *Type A Behavior and Your Heart,* Drs. Meyer and Friedman describe the Type A personality. Such people are common in the U.S.A., representing about 50 percent of the population.
Type A behavior is aggressive, competitive, concerned about position and accomplishments. There is a sense of insecurity and impatience, and a tendency to brag about past achievements.

In men with Type A personalities, heart disease was three times more common than the more relaxed Type B personality. Most Type A were between thirty and forty years of age when they suffered their first heart atack. They were often prediabetic, and had clotting abnormalities in the blood.

The heart is sensitive to stress hormones released by the adrenal glands. The "cardiac conducting system," the inner lining of the heart, is responsible for synchronizing the heartbeat, allowing blood to be pumped to the vital organs such as the brain. A heart attack may damage the conducting system, causing the heartbeat to go wildly out of control. These irregular heartbeats are termed "arrhythmias," the most dangerous of which is "ventricular fibrillation." In this condition the heart muscle quivers without producing any pumping effort, and death generally occurs within minutes. The victim of an acute heart attack (myocardial infarction) is more in danger of dying of an arrhythmia than from actual damage to the heart muscle itself.

In a study of one hundred and seventeen patients

who died suddenly and unexpectedly, it was found that many had been under intense psychological stress. Usually there had been a significant, even overwhelming, loss, such as the death of a spouse or child. Death generally occurred within an hour of bad news. Sudden death has also resulted from times of joy, such as a reunion with a close relative.

Heart Spasms and Chest Pain. The heart muscle receives its blood supply via the coronary arteries. A few years ago it was discovered these vessels can go into spasms, producing the pain of a heart attack. These spasms tend to occur at times of stress. Unlike the angina pain of blocked coronary arteries, which occurs during physical activity, "spasm" angina may occur at rest. This is called *variant* or *Prinzmetal's* angina.

Diabetes. Diane Gordon was a normal, healthy twenty-two-year-old college senior. During the school year she noticed she felt increasing fatigue, and she drank large quantities of water. When she lost weight and became seriously dehydrated, her parents grew concerned. At first they had attributed her condition to the hectic pace of senior activities. Now they were alarmed at her appearance and the fact that it was difficult to arouse her from sleep one morning.

A trip to the family doctor revealed Diane had diabetes. Daily injections of insulin would be needed, which she dreaded. Diane was resentful of her new medical condition and concealed it from her friends. Her diet was restrictive and embarrassing, and she was afraid others, especially her fiancé, would discover she was diabetic. (Since her grandmother had had diabetes, Diane was afraid the condition was hereditary.) At school parties she ate and drank as much as others and frequently skipped her insulin.

Gradually her wasted appearance became alarming,

and Diane's life became miserable. She was depressed, but tried to pretend nothing was wrong. As graduation approached, she grew even more frantic about concealing her diabetes from others.

Diane lost weight again, and one night she grew restless, went to her room, and became delirious with fever. Within minutes she lapsed into a coma and was unresponsive. An ambulance took her directly to the emergency room at the hospital, and she arrived in critical condition. She was in diabetic keto-acidosis and a coma, a life-threatening complication requiring intensive medical care. Fortunately, within a few days she regained consciousness and was well on the way to recovery.

Several long discussions with her doctor revealed her denial of her illness and failure to conform to her diet, but this did not seem to explain why she went into a coma. Finally Diane admitted that she feared her fiancé would reject her because of the diabetes, since it was hereditary and could affect their future children. Diane's problem with poor control of diabetes stemmed from her inappropriate response to the stress of her fears.

The pancreas is the "target organ" in diabetes, and is responsible for manufacturing insulin, a hormone needed to metabolize sugar. The insulin-producing cells are called beta cells. Diabetes is thought to be caused by loss of the beta cells, either because of genetic inherited factors, or because the person's own immune system produces antibodies which destroy the beta cells. The individual becomes unable to make enough insulin, and diabetes results.

At times of severe stress, especially in a major life crisis, overworked beta cells are required to manufacture more insulin, but are unable to do so. Stress is the trigger event, and an already susceptible individual finds himself facing diabetes.

The life of the diabetic is a careful balance of caloric intake, exercise, and regulation of insulin injections. Stress can lead to hormonal changes, making it more difficult to control blood sugar. Children exposed to severe family conflicts lose control of their diabetes more easily, and can develop life-threatening complications. So treatment often consists of medication, diet, and stress management.

Headaches. The most common cause of human suffering and pain, aside from hunger and cold, is a headache. The pain of a headache can be excruciating, continuous, and debilitating. Fortunately, most people do not experience the most severe form of headache, but there are few who have not suffered from head pain at one time or another in their lives.

Migraines are the most common type of headache. They produce a severe, throbbing pain, usually accompanied by nausea and vomiting. A migraine attack begins with gradually increasing pain and, possibly, warning symptoms such as flashing lights or blind spots. The sufferer often seeks the solitude of a dark, quiet room, waiting for hours or even days until the headache subsides.

Trigger events include stress, bright lights, glare, certain foods or alcohol, fatigue, and hormonal changes of the menstrual period in women. There is a strong genetic tendency for this disorder.

Tension Headaches feel like a tight band around the head, and the scalp is often sore and tingly. These headaches tend to occur every day, and are worse during stress or emotional upsets. But the sufferer rarely sees the connection between stress and the headaches. Since a tension headache may trigger a migraine, there often is a mixture of the two headaches in the same patient.

Cluster Headaches cause excruciating pain. Women

who have undergone the experience of both childbirth and cluster headaches have said the headache is the worse of the two experiences. People have been known to commit suicide during these attacks. This little-known headache disorder deserves wider attention, especially since treatment is usually very helpful.

Cluster headaches begin as a driving pain behind one eye. Within moments the pain reaches a crescendo. The person may pace about nervously, even screaming and writhing in pain, beating his head against the floor. The eye on the side of the headache becomes red and tearful. Frequently, because of nasal discharge and congestion, these headaches are attributed to sinus problems, but this is an erroneous conclusion. Attacks of cluster headaches may occur with clocklike regularity at exactly the same time each day.

Mary Alt's headaches were getting worse, so she went to her doctor. All examinations and tests were negative, and attempts to treat the problem were frustrating. A specialist was consulted; he diagnosed migraine. Mary's family doctor spent time talking to her, trying to find out as much as possible about her symptoms. Her mother had suffered from "sick headaches," much like hers, and a teenage daughter was beginning to have similar attacks. When the headache reached its peak, Mary frequently passed out from the pain. After four or five days in bed, the headache would gradually go away. Until recently she would have only one or two severe headache attacks per year. Now they were occurring several times a month. Why the worsening pattern?

During one of her visits to the doctor, Mary brought her daughter along. As they were talking, both Mary and her doctor confessed that they did not know why the headaches were becoming more severe. When the daughter heard this, she sat up and said, "I know,

Mother. The headaches got worse when you started your own business."

Mary had not seen the connection, but when she heard it, she knew it was true. She had started an interior design business in her spare time, and it had grown beyond all expectations. She was much in demand by her clients and found little time for her family, which upset her husband. In addition, her income now exceeded his, causing further conflict. When Mary decided to discontinue her business and devote time to her home and family, her headaches subsided.

Summary

Illness results from a combination of natural or medical causes, stress, and spiritual problems. Stress commonly serves as a "trigger" event, pushing a person who may be overly tired and emotionally drained into physical illness.

Often, the type of illness a person suffers depends on what areas of weakness already exist within his body. For example, someone who has a "problem stomach" is a prime candidate for an ulcer. This weakness becomes the "target" area where an illness can set in quickly. Many serious illnesses are worsened by stress, including heart disease, diabetes, ulcers, and severe headaches. Therefore, effective treatment should include stress management techniques as well as medication and physical health-centered instructions.

Ten
Coping with the Unexpected
The Stress of Unavoidable Adversity

"Here on earth you will have many trials and sorrows"
(John 16:33).
"Forewarned is half-armed" (Latin proverb).

No doubt you've heard each of these quotations, the
one made by Jesus and the other a familiar proverb, at
some time in your life. However, if you're familiar with
the Latin proverb, you've probably already spotted the
error. The correct version is "forewarned is *fore*armed!"
But while that may be an accurate translation of the
Latin, it is not an accurate reflection of reality. An
explicit, painstakingly detailed forewarning might help a
person meet a predictable challenge or avoid a problem,
but it won't help him cope with unavoidable adversity.

What would you really do if tragedy struck? How
would you hold up? If it is true that being forewarned
does not automatically lead to the ability to cope, then
how can we become forearmed or equipped to combat
the destructive impact of unexpected tragedy?

A Survivor's Secret. There was strain in his voice even in
remembering the horror. "I was an emotional wreck.
One and a half hours before they would come in, I was

in literal terror. Four of them would have to force me down, and they stuck a washrag in my mouth to drown out my screams. Eventually I passed out from the pain as they ripped the dressings off my exposed flesh, day after day, two times a day . . . and it went on for six weeks. It was a procedure they had to use after they amputated my legs . . . the flesh had to heal from the inside out. And the pain had crossed my point of tolerance."

Three years after a disastrous plane crash near the frigid summit of Mount Columbia, on the edge of the black timbered Rocky Mountains, Steve Smart reminisced about his unanticipated crisis. We were discussing the fact that his story would be written about in the book, *Discipline That Can't Fail* (Mott Media, 1984), and that his tragedy would be an inspiration to others. The account of Steve's experience follows:

"His [Smart's] story, and the story of his companions, was carried on the front page of successive issues of The Denver Post *on December 30 and December 31 of 1981, beginning with the headline on December 30, '"Miracle" Rescue Saves Four Texans Five Days After Mountain Crash.' Excerpts from the story read:*

" 'Deciding to make one last attempt after five days of searching, rescuers following a weak radio signal trudged through seven foot deep snow Tuesday afternoon and discovered four injured persons huddled in the wreckage of a small plane at the eleven thousand, six hundred foot level of Mount Columbia.

" 'One pilot-doctor told The Denver Post *it was a miracle that the victims survived hurricane-force winds earlier this week which caused a wind-chill factor reaching sixty degrees below zero in the Colorado Rockies one hundred air miles southwest of Denver. A fifth victim—the pilot—had walked from the plane after it crashed on*

Christmas Eve to seek help. There was no trace of him, the rescue party reported. . . .'

"In the story the next day, the real drama was revealed by another survivor, Patricia Meeks: '. . . After we landed (on the afternoon of Christmas Eve) the weather really got bad, snowing and blowing snow . . . sometimes we couldn't even see tops of the trees.' Mrs. Meeks added that at other times they could see circling planes and helicopters but probably couldn't be seen because of the snow covering their plane at the edge of the tree line.

"'When the rescuers arrived . . . Mrs. Meeks was reading the Bible,' Smart said, 'at the passage as to why God lets us suffer . . . we never gave up hope, never. We just made our peace up there, and if somebody wanted to rescue us, we'd consent to serving Jesus here, and if they didn't we'd just join him.'

"Perhaps the real miracle of the dramatic rescue was that Steve Smart's picture, accompanied by his dynamic testimony in large boldface type, was carried, along with the rest of the story, on the front page of The Denver Post!

"But were Smart's words merely an expected, uncontrollable emotional outpouring of relief upon being rescued—a kind of temporary 'spiritual high' that is often encountered in crisis, but that just as often vanishes when the immediate crisis is over? Or were they genuine evidence that there are, indeed, Christians like Steve Smart who lean on the Word of God and who are able to share their faith with others in the time of their most challenging ordeal?

"Almost exactly one year later, on December 26, 1982, Steve Smart, whose legs had been amputated below the knee because of frostbite complications, was pictured and quoted in The Denver Post in an anniversary story of the miracle rescue. He again provided an unwavering affirmation of his relationship with a personal God. And in 1982 it was Patricia Meeks' picture and accompanying testimony, in boldface type, which graced the front page of

The Denver Post, *highlighting a headline which read,* *'Faith, Hope—Two Legacies of Rockie Plane Crash.'*

"'There is some reason why we didn't all die up there,'* Mrs. Meeks asserted.

"Even a year later, the faith of two Christians, one of whom lost his legs, and the other who lost her husband, remained bold and unwavering—even stronger in the face of adversity.

"Now it was three years later. Three years of struggles for Steve Smart. But his Christian walk was more solid than ever.

" 'If the accident were to happen now, I would trust the Lord, according to Psalm 31. If we accept Jesus, we have to accept all of him, just as he accepts all of us. He's promised that if we surrender ourselves to him, he will take total control . . . Whatever happens . . . we cannot see around the corner. He could be using something in our life, although we may view it as a crisis or a tragedy. Our physical existence becomes less and less important each day. We are here for fellowship with God.

" 'Anything that happens to me I can thank him regardless of what it is, because he has a plan for my life. Psalm 31 means to me that, "Lord, today is your day." Sure, pressures are always with us, but the only time that I experience tension is when I enter into fearful thoughts without the Lord with me. I have absolutely no worry. If somebody told me I had a terminal illness, I'd say "Okay, Lord, you have something worked out; who are you trying to reach—show me." Stress management? Without Christ, it's impossible. With him, you can't fail.' "

A "Survivor" of Another Kind. Ronald Hulse's wife had no enemies. In the sleepy rural Indiana countryside near Argos, a town of about fifteen hundred, a stranger, suspicious looking or not, would have been noticed. But no stranger had been seen. And there was no rational explanation for the brutal assault upon, and murder of, Ronald's wife, Darlene, who, early one morning, was dragged out of her home in full view of their three daughters, ages eight, six, and one, and whose lifeless body was found in a field the next day.

Special correspondent Beth Divine, in a story headlined on the front page of the August 21, 1984, Sunday edition of the *Indianapolis Star*, focused on the faith of Ron Hulse as the theme of her poignant story. She quoted his musings as he grappled to understand this irrational and incomprehensible act of violence:

"I couldn't imagine going through this alone," Ron said. "I just know it's his will. Darlene was ready. I'm ready whenever he wants to take me. It's just that. Otherwise I'd be a basket case."

Divine wrote that Ron was all too aware of the grim facts of the case. He knew of his wife's pleading for her children, the graphic evidence in his house of her beating, the fact that his children witnessed the abduction. Nevertheless, his spiritual reserves gave him an indestructible base in which he found peace of mind.

"Someday we'll see her again," Ron said. "The girls don't even care to go to the cemetery. They say, 'Mommy's not there. It won't do any good.' The bottom line is I couldn't imagine someone who isn't a Christian going through this. . . . I just place myself and my daughters in the Lord's hands. We'll make it through . . . Time will heal all."

Other Tragedies: Other Triumphs. Steve Smart and Ron Hulse—bulwarks of faith. But can it be argued that they are rare cases? That their stories are isolated examples, and their faith-inspired capacity to manage stress is the result of unattainable qualities that are out of reach for the average person? Are such stories as theirs so infrequent that one has to scan the wire news services that cover the world to find similar accounts?

The following facts speak for themselves:

The date: December 20, 1984.
The place: Denver, Colorado.

Jim Matthews did not suspect that anything was wrong. He had returned home at 9:30 P.M. from seventeen-year-old daughter Jennifer's basketball game. He was caught up in the holiday mood, and called a cheery greeting to twelve-year-old daughter Jonelle, who had participated in a Christmas concert and been dropped off at home by friends an hour earlier. Deciding to make good use of a few spare minutes, he wrapped a Christmas present, addressed a few cards, and took note of a telephone message Jonelle had scribbled about forty-five mintues earlier.

How does one describe "knowing doubt"—the sudden thrust of awareness that rolls from the solar plexus to the throat like a huge lead ball, and slams itself into unwilling consciousness like a hostile intruder? Jonelle! She hadn't returned his greeting! And suddenly parts of a threatening picture came together in a flood of frightening speculation: The television set had been on when he walked into the house; Jonelle's shoes and socks were next to her favorite TV chair; the quartz heater was plugged in. Denying his emerging panic, Jim raced through the house . . . and his knowing doubt became a certainty—Jonelle was missing!

The most difficult part, Jim recalled, was when he and his wife, Gloria, and their daughter, Jennifer, sat together, stifling their tears, to open their presents from Jonelle. At first they were going to wait until she was returned to them. But after that first night five nights earlier, when their hope was fueled by the teams of police officers and FBI agents who took hundreds of photographs and fanned out to pursue every lead, they felt the need for some contact with Jonelle. After carefully—almost reverently—placing their presents to Jonelle in her room, they lovingly opened their gifts from her.

And now it was Easter. Almost four months had passed; months when it seemed that their very hearts were being torn apart. Months of terrifying imagination, bitter tears, and imploring prayer. Months made bearable only because of hundreds of fellow Christians who covered the Matthew family in a tide of love, and who continued to buoy their spirits by surrounding them with prayer and concern.

Then, on Easter morning, 1985, Jim Matthews shared his family's strength with thousands of people on "20/20 Insight," a Denver radio talk-show. Their story would edify thousands of other believers through rebroadcasts on Christian radio throughout North America. People nationwide heard Jim say:

"Very seldom are people able to receive God's love through others as our family has. We are almost privileged to be on the receiving end of this, to feel the concern and love of other Christians. We have to realize that God will have victory. We have to realize that God's timing is perfect. God's glory will be magnified in this situation, bringing souls to Christ, which is what we are here for. . . We have two choices: We can let the situation engulf us, or rise above it and glorify God and help others. . . . The tomb is empty and the Savior is risen."

The date: February 15, 1985.
The place: Conifer, Colorado.

The Rocky Mountain News, in a story by medical writer Pamela Avery, unfolded the events leading to the untimely death of nine-year-old Jennifer Wise, whose one-year struggle with leukemia provided an inspiring portrayal of "the faith of a child." Jennifer had endured debilitating and unsuccessful chemotherapy for a year. When faced with more of this, she interrupted her parents' discussion of her treatment with a penetrating question: "Don't I have a say in what to do? I would rather die and go to heaven."

Jennifer's astoundingly mature faith manifested itself in other ways as well. In anticipation of her death, she distributed her stuffed animal collection to church friends and to her younger siblings. She agreed to carry to heaven greetings to various Scripture personalities from her Sunday school friends. She compared a scriptural account of a healing with her own persisting illness and failure to recover, and apprised her father, Joe Wise, of the fact that "it was God's will" to heal the woman with the issue of blood, but not to heal Jennifer. And she urged her parents to "pray, pray," each time she choked for her breath in the later stages of her illness.

Jennifer's mother ended the interview saying, "Jennifer had her own faith. I am convinced that God gave her special sensitivity from two years on so she could handle her illness."

The date: October 10, 1982.
The place: Grand Junction, Colorado.

Another front-page story of triumphant faith overcoming the onslaught of continuing adversity, bannered the Sunday edition of *The Denver Post* on October 10, 1982. Jeff and Suzie Wilkinson's idyllic life as a ranching family on Colorado's western slope of the Rockies had been untouched by even the minor stresses of unpaid bills. Then tragedy struck: The Wilkinsons' youngest child, Hannah, was sucked into a rain-engorged irrigation pipe, and carried underground by a torrent of water for eighty feet, until, twenty minutes later, frantic neighbors and her horrified father pulled her from the clutches of death after tearing up huge sections of earth and pipe to get to her. Six weeks later, she remained in a coma; her prognosis for survival was good. But the chances of full recovery without brain damage were poor.

Despite the agony of uncertainty and a discouraging prognosis, the Wilkinsons' ability to cope was inspiring. *Denver Post* staff writer Tom Coakley interviewed Jeff Wilkinson, reporting that, "for strength, the couple has turned often to the Bible and what God says about trusting in him and about the value of tribulation in life."

"We're holding up all right," Jeff Wilkinson said. "You see, the thing about this is that the Lord loves her more than I do. At first that was a hard pill for me to choke down, but he does. The Lord lends you a child just like he lends you your life."

The stress of sudden adversity had been vanquished by the Wilkinsons. They were not forewarned; but *they* were forearmed.

The date: October 24, 1982.
The place: Lakewood, Colorado.

Three hundred people packed a small church in suburban Denver for the funeral of three boys whose lives were tragically ended in an inferno which engulfed the mobile home in which they slept.

A forty-six-point headline, "Faith Cheers Bereaved Mother," dominated *The Metro News'* front page and summarized the eloquent confession of faith of Jacki Neutzman, the mother of two of the boys. Her two-year-old and four-year-old sons had parted from her for the last time three days before to visit their father.

Gary Delsohn, a *Denver Post* staff writer, captured the essence of the steadfast trust of the tragedy-stricken mother in the record of her testimony at the funeral:

"These tears are tears of joy for God. I trust him so much that I know if there was a better way for my babies in this life, he would have left them. But he wanted them with him."

Delsohn also cited highlights of the sermon of Rev. Joseph Meyer, whose message of hope explained the mother's astounding faith:

"Grief for a Christian is never the same as despair. The Christian teaching about death is that it is only a temporary separation. If we have accepted Jesus as our Savior, we know when we die we will go with the little children to our Lord, and we will be united with our Christian loved ones.

"The Christian perspective on all life is that it comes from God."

Remember the question about whether the ability to endure the stress of tragic adversity was an isolated, rarely observed phenomenon? The compelling examples of the Matthews, the Wises, the Wilkersons, and Jacki Neutzman— examples of triumph in tragedy—all occurred within a relatively limited time span. They were not rare and isolated cases. They all occurred in one limited geographical area. Indeed, each situation took place within less than a day's drive from Denver, Colorado. They were not widely dispersed over vast expanses of geography, necessitating a twenty-four-hour-a-day, seven-day-a-week scrutinizing of the worldwide news services!

In each of these tragedies, the survivors did not have the benefit of being forearmed, or even half-armed, by a forewarning. Calamity swooped quickly, like some menacing bird of prey, and in a sudden moment it seized in its soul-tearing talons the once tragedy-free existence of these people.

But the survivors became victors, not victims. They

overcame, rather than being overcome. They sought no solace in the synthetic escape of chemicals, the emotional death of psychological breakdown, or in suicide. They all had something in common—something that is necessary to complete the Scripture reference with which this chapter began. Remember the reference? Jesus said: "Here on earth you will have many trials and sorrows."

His words are certainly a forewarning; but the reference is incomplete, for it also includes a fore*arming*—a confidence-building, character-strengthing, faith-inspiring fact for overcoming the stress of unexpected adversity:

"I have told you all this so you will have peace of heart and mind. *Here on earth you will have many trials and sorrows,* but cheer up, for I have overcome the world" (John 16:33, emphasis added).

God's Armor for Adversity:
Suffering, pain, sorrow, grief—these are inescapable experiences of life (see 1 Thessalonians 3:2-4). But God has also said, in Psalm 91:4, that his faithful promises are our armor. The Scriptures provide insight for us about the protection we have when our spirits are assailed by adversity. With dynamic power and explosive impact God's Word declares:

1. That even when we are victimized by intentional evil, God intervenes in the situation and blesses us through it (Genesis 50:20).
2. That our desire to know the "why" of our adversity is a part of the agony of our human condition. It was a part of the agony of Job, the model of faith in the face of adversity (Job 10:1, 2), and a part of the agony of Jesus, our perfect role model.

3. That our sorrow is temporary, but our joy will be permanent (Psalm 30:5; 31:24).

4. That, because of God's love for us and his absolute care for us, we need not fear "accidents," for God is completely sovereign over our lives, completely in charge of anything that can affect us and completely concerned for the well-being of those who love him. (See Psalm 31:14, 15; 34:20.)

5. That we need not fear calamity, disaster, or the terrors of the night (Psalm 91).

6. That God is fully aware of our sufferings, and that they are a part of his plan for us as he leads us to eternal life (Jeremiah 24:4-7; 1 Thessalonians 3:3, 4).

7. That we and our loved ones will emerge victorious in a state of incomprehensible splendor, which will enable us to put the sufferings of this life into a comprehensible perspective—a perspective we can now only imperfectly understand (Romans 8:18; 1 Corinthians 13:12).

8. That all things work together for good to them that love God (Romans 8:28; Philippians 1:19).

9. That as irrational and unbelievable as it may seem, we can rejoice in the Lord and trust him no matter what happens because what God has prepared for us and where he is leading us are inexpressibly, unbelievably wonderful (Psalm 34:1; 1 Corinthians 2:9; and Philippians 3:1).

Preparing for Adversity. "The thing about a crisis is that you cannot, in the *middle* of the crisis, prepare yourself for it." The intermittent fading in and out that had been affecting the long distance telephone connection between Denver and Winnipeg, Manitoba, twelve hundred miles to the northeast, for the radio talk show interview did not interfere with the transmission of

Cliff Derksen's penetrating insight. Here was another survivor who had experienced incredible success in coping with crisis.

When Cliff and his wife, Wilma, were interviewed on "20/20 Insight," (along with Jim Matthews), they shared their victory in coping with the agony of the abduction and subsequent murder of their twelve-year-old daughter, Candace. Because the radio show was carried on a secular station, these two families' stories of suffering, and triumph in Jesus Christ, brought to a secular audience undeniable testimony of the power of a risen Savior. The Derksens told that, from the beginning of the search until the discovery of their daughter's body, they turned the situation over to God. They were able to manage the crisis because they had been close to Jesus Christ as a family. They had steeped themselves in the Word of God, worshipped and shared together, *before the crisis ever occurred.* They had put on the armor of God—prayer, worship, Scripture study, and dedication to Christ—before the battle had ever begun!

And from Jim Matthews, who sat stoically in the radio studio while an international search continued for his missing twelve-year-old daughter, came this triumphant declaration: "It's sometimes hard to be with the Lord when things are going good. But stay with him in the good times and you'll stay with him in the bad times!" As Jesus said, "All who listen to my instructions and follow them are wise, like a man who builds his house on solid rock. Though the rain comes in torrents, and the floods rise and the storm winds beat against his house, it won't collapse, for it is built on rock" (Matthew 7:24, 25).

How, then does one prepare for adversity? God has provided the way.

"That is why God says in the Scriptures, 'Awake, O sleeper, and rise up from the dead; and Christ shall give

you light.' So be careful how you act; these are difficult days. Don't be fools; be wise: make the most of every opportunity you have for doing good. Don't act thoughtlessly, but try to find out and do whatever the Lord wants you to. Don't drink too much wine, for many evils lie along that path; be filled with the Holy Spirit, and controlled by him. Talk with each other much about the Lord, quoting psalms and hymns and singing sacred songs, making music in your hearts to the Lord. Always give thanks for everything to our God and Father in the name of our Lord Jesus Christ" (Ephesians 5:14-20.)

"So we must listen very carefully to the truths we have heard, or we may drift away from them" (Hebrews 2:1).

"And those whose faith has made them good in God's sight must live by faith, trusting him in everything. Otherwise, if they shrink back, God will have no pleasure in them" (Hebrews 10:38).

"Keep your eyes on Jesus, our leader and instructor. He was willing to die a shameful death on the cross because of the joy he knew would be his afterwards; and now he sits in the place of honor by the throne of God" (Hebrews 12:2).

"If you want to know what God wants you to do, ask him, and he will gladly tell you, for he is always ready to give a bountiful supply of wisdom to all who ask him; he will not resent it" (James 1:5).

"But if anyone keeps looking steadily into God's law for free men, he will not only remember it but he will do what it says, and God will greatly bless him in everything he does (James 1:25).

"If you will humble yourselves under the mighty hand of God, in his good time he will lift you up. Let him have all your worries and cares, for he is always thinking about you and watching everything that concerns you" (1 Peter 5:6, 7).

The same key to managing stress emerges, regardless of the situation: Immerse yourself in God's Word. There are no clearer instructions on how to do this than those found in Deuteronomy 6:6-9:

*"And you must think constantly about these command-
ments I am giving you today. You must teach them to your
children and talk about them when you are at home or out
for a walk; at bedtime and the first thing in the morning.
Tie them on your finger, wear them on your forehead, and
write them on the doorposts of your house!"*

Some powerful Scriptures that are especially helpful in managing the stress of unavoidable adversity are listed here. If committed to memory, they will become an impregnable armor in time of trouble:

> *Proverbs 3:25*
> *Proverbs 3:56*
> *Proverbs 29:26*
> *Isaiah 41:10*
> *Matthew 6:31-34*
> *Matthew 10:28-31*
> *Romans 5:3-5*
> *Romans 8:28*
> *Romans 8:31*
> *Romans 8:38, 39*
> *Philippians 4:6, 7, 13*
> *2 Timothy 2:13*

It is only through the power of the Word of God that faith, the only armor which can withstand the onslaught of tragic adversity, is constructed. Faith is inherent in yet another old saying:

*"Fear knocked at the door.
Faith answered.
Nobody was there."*

Eleven
Defeating the Failure Phobia

The Teacher Who Got an "F"

By any measure of teaching performance, he was a failure. "Process criteria"—the measurement of *how* teaching is done—would have blasted his methods. In the first place, some of his lectures were obviously vague, so much so that even his best students had to come to him after the lecture period to ask him to explain the lesson. In their frustration, they asked him why he used teaching methods which caused confusion. He admitted, not without some impatience, that he had done so deliberately—that his teaching methods were chosen specifically so that some of his listeners would not understand!

The application of "product criteria," on the other hand—measuring of *what* was taught by student performance on examinations—rendered an equally unfavorable judgment of his teaching. He had worked with a relatively small group of motivated learners, but the whole class flunked the mid-term exam. One of his students dropped out of class, never to return.

His personal credentials, as well as the content of his curriculum, were also under attack. Although he had, in his preteen years, impressed officials at the most prestigious educational institution in the country with the fact that he was obviously gifted, his qualifications to teach were later severely questioned. Both his education and what he taught simply did not adhere to institutional requirements. Most of the people who heard him teach allied themselves with the establishment and either tacitly or overtly approved initiating legal proceedings against him. Had current laws been in effect then, he probably could have won a suit on the basis of deprivation of his civil rights. Unfortunately, politics back then interfered with the pursuit of justice. He was forcibly prevented from teaching, and labeled a danger to society. He never taught again, other than through example. And when he died, he was penniless and disgraced.

His name? Jesus Christ!

What Is Failure? According to the *American Heritage Dictionary,* failure is "the condition or fact of not achieving the desired end or ends."

Few things are more perplexing to a Christian than a situation in which he diligently and sincerely asks God's blessing upon an endeavor, only to watch his cherished venture fall with a mighty crash in abject failure. But whether or not the stress of failure leads to distress depends upon a person's definition of failure.

This chapter began with an account of a man whose life, by one set of standards, was a dismal failure. But by another set of standards, his life was the most astounding success the world has ever known. It is obvious, then, that failure is a matter of definition. An erroneous definition of failure will lead to inescapable distress; an accurate definition will lead to well-managed stress.

Consider the following scriptural facts:

God's primary concern for you is your eternal salvation (Jeremiah 24:4-8).

God's primary purpose for your life is to serve others (Ephesians 2:10).

God has promised to guide you, help you make the right decisions, and to direct your paths (Proverbs 3:5, 6).

The best blessing God has for you is his Holy Spirit, who will help you fulfill your purpose in time, and to achieve your goal in eternity (Luke 11:13).

Since God has promised to lead and direct you, and since his best blessing is his Holy Spirit, then it makes sense that the paths on which you find yourself are those to which God has directed you, and they will always lead to a Holy Spirit-generated faith and steadfastness in Christ (Psalm 25:12-14).

Increased faith and steadfastness in Christ are of immeasurably greater value than any material blessing. These, then are the *ultimate* measure of success, and any experiences which lead to this increased faith and steadfastness must be successful experiences.

It is clear, then, that for the Christian, since *every* experience has been promised by God to be a God-directed experience that will lead to success in his major purpose of increased spiritual growth, faith, and steadfastness, then apparent failure is exactly that: *apparent* failure.

Lest we doubt this conclusion, further clarification is provided in the Gospel of Luke. The disciples, having rejoiced over Jesus' triumphal entry into Jerusalem, had every reason to accept a temporal definition of "success." After all, the people had acclaimed Jesus as king and he had accepted their adulation. And a king's inner circle of friends always enjoyed special treatment, so they were sure that they'd really "made it." But Jesus was quick to dispel their false notions of success. Speaking of the end times and of their future, he said, "You will be dragged into synagogues and prisons and before kings and governors for my Name's sake. But as a result, the Messiah will be widely known and honored" (Luke 21:12, 13).

Clearly, success was not to be measured by conventional standards. What normally would be considered as the most catastrophic failure was really success when measured against a different standard: The standard of spreading Christ's Gospel! Apparent failure. Real success.

The same definition of success was asserted by the apostle Paul, in Philippians 1:12-14. Fettered with chains, taunted by jealous competitors, and facing the very real possibility of an imminent and violent death, Paul's deep, Holy Spirit-inspired faith led him to a brilliant insight into the whole concept of apparent failure and real success:

"And I want you to know this, dear brothers: Everything that has happened to me here has been a great boost in getting out the Good News concerning Christ. For everyone around here, including all the soldiers over at the barracks, knows that I am in chains simply because I am a Christian. And because of my imprisonment many of the Christians here seem to have lost their fear of chains! Somehow my patience has encouraged them and they have become more and more bold in telling others about Christ.

"The Good News about Christ is being preached and I am glad. I am going to keep on being glad, for I know that as you pray for me, and as the Holy Spirit helps me, this is all going to turn out for my good" (Philippians 1:12-14, 18, 19).

Paul never lost sight of the fact that, regardless of what seemed to be failure, real success always remained with the child of God. "Whatever happens," he told the Philippian Christians, "be glad in the Lord" (Philippians 3:1). "Always be thankful no matter what happens," he encouraged the Christians in Thessalonica (1 Thessalonians 5:18). "And we know that all things work together for good to them that love God," he told the Roman Christians (Romans 8:28, KJV). Apparent failure. Real success. A matter of definition.

The Failure Phobia: Dispelling Some Misconceptions
One major fact needs to be recognized: For the Christian, there is no fear of failure. If I ask the Lord to bless my efforts, I am, essentially, relinquishing my right to determine the specific shape of the outcome of my efforts. Therefore, I should suffer no distress, even if things do not turn out as I had anticipated or hoped. God is in charge, and he will see that the outcome of my endeavors enhance my achieving his purposes and goals for me. There can be no failure. And, for the Christian who "seeks first the kingdom of God and his righteousness," where there is no failure, there is no fear of failure.

"Pray as Hard as You Can—and Row for the Shore." The Russian proverb above challenges a widely-held misconception: If God is in charge, then he'll take care of everything. So the well-meaning Christian refuses to pursue solutions to problems, or to strive to attain specific objectives. Much distress results from this passivity of spirit, which not only flouts common sense, but disregards the scriptural guideline of Ecclesiastes 9:10: "Whatsoever thy hand findeth to do, do it with thy might" (KJV).

The examples of misguided, distress-inducing "trust" are rife. For example, one Christian school pays its dedicated teachers only 60 percent of their salaries as a result of a funds crunch. The school refuses to try to solve its economic crisis, because, after all, "God will provide." Another example is the young man or woman who "waits on the Lord" for a job and suffers financial distress, instead of going out to look for the job which is just around the corner. Or the well-intentioned person who "hasn't heard God speak" about the type of ministry he should enter, so he ignores the muted cries in his immediate environment for help.

Does the Bible support such passivity and advocate it as trust? The actions of Nehemiah and Jesus provide an answer.

God had burned a desire into Nehemiah's heart to rebuild the walls of Jerusalem. This task was blessed with supernatural intervention from the time of its inception until the time it was nearly finished. But suddenly Nehemiah faced a deadly threat to the completion of his God-sanctioned work. When the wall was only half-completed, Nehemiah discovered that his enemies were preparing to lead an army against Jerusalem, to destroy him and his people. Before we look at Nehemiah's response to this threat, it might help to remember that:

Nehemiah knew, without a doubt, that his calling had been put into his heart by God himself (see Nehemiah 2:12, 18).

He knew that God had caused King Artaxerxes to be kind to him, and to be extraordinarily generous in giving him building materials (see Nehemiah 2:8).

So Nehemiah had every reason to believe that God, who had created his desire for the work, caused him to find favor with the king, and provided him with the protection and means to do the work, would naturally confuse and disperse his enemies.

In view of the staggering evidence of God's divine intervention in Nehemiah's work, it seemed more than reasonable for Nehemiah to tell his people, "Don't worry. God will provide." Then he and his people could have blithely—and foolishly—neglected their responsibility to protect themselves, preoccupying themselves instead with finishing the wall.

Well, in essence, that's exactly what Nehemiah *did* say to his people! "Don't be afraid! Remember the Lord who is great and glorious." But he didn't stop there. "Fight for your friends," he went on, "your families, and your homes!" (Nehemiah 4:14). Nehemiah's attitude was perfectly clear as he related what was done in response to the ominous warnings of a deadly force waiting to explode against him and his people. He told his people of the situation, and then outlined a battle strategy; "But *we prayed to our God, and guarded the city day and night to protect ourselves*" (Nehemiah 4:9). This, then, should be our response to troubles: "Pray as though everything depends on God; work as though everything depends on you."

Maximal Trust: Maximal Effort. If anyone ever had a right to passivity and the expectation that God would bring everything to him, it was Jesus. His life was the fulfillment of prophecy after prophecy. And when Christ approached Jerusalem, another prophecy, "Tell Jerusalem her King is coming to her, riding humbly on a donkey's colt" (Matthew 21:5), was about to be fulfilled.

But where was the donkey's colt? Here was the Messiah, the King of Kings and Lord of Lords, who had been perfectly obedient to his heavenly Father and done everything in accordance with his Father's will . . . here he was, waiting on the outskirts of Jerusalem, ready to "bring to final completion the plan of salvation"—and there was no donkey. Wouldn't it be reasonable to expect that "God will provide" and that a donkey, born for this most auspicious moment in history, would miraculously materialize, and trot eagerly and obediently onto the scene?

But instead of passively waiting for this phenomenon,

we are told that Jesus *sent his disciples forth* to *get* a colt and a donkey. He told them what to say, and who to say it to. And the disciples did indeed go forth and get the donkey and colt, and bring the animals to him (Matthew 21:1-7).

Without a doubt, God *did* provide the donkey, but Jesus initiated the necessary action to avail himself of what God had provided.

"We prayed to our God and guarded the city day and night to protect ourselves." Nehemiah's strategy is the perfect metaphor for managing the stress of problem-solving: Maximal trust equals maximal effort. And the result is maximal achievement and *minimal stress.*

Defusing the Time Bomb

Time-stress is another stress that is an ever-present source of possible problems. There always seems to be either too much or too little time. It passes too quickly or too slowly. Fortunately, time-stress is the one stress that we can control the most and have the most opportunity to manage.

Basically, time-stress occurs: (1) when things don't go according to our schedule; (2) when we have too many activities for a certain time; (3) when we are too early or late for an event and have to waste time waiting in line, in traffic, or elsewhere; or (4) when we allot too little time necessary to complete a task.

The fallout of each of these potentially explosive circumstances possesses distress-causing consequences. But they can be defused through scriptural insights. Let's look at each in turn.

When Things Don't Go According to Our Schedule.
Remember the story of Lazarus in John 11? Mary and Martha had sent an urgent message to Jesus, telling him, "Sir, your good friend is very, very sick." They were desperate, but they knew how busy Jesus was,

that huge crowds milled about him constantly. They knew how tired he was, and that he needed times away from the crowds to try to rest and refresh his strength.

Mary and Martha's message was pointed in its simplicity. They did not ask Jesus to come at once; they were acutely sensitive to the demands on his time. But implicit in their brief message was their plea, "Hurry! We need you now! This is serious or we would not have bothered you with it!"

With mounting desperation they watched for Jesus. They knew how much he loved Lazarus, and they were sure that he would understand the critical nature of their request. But he did not appear. As the hours passed and sunlight turned to darkness, they watched their brother's condition deteriorate, and their emotions ran wild through desperation, urgency, frustration, and panic! But there was still no Jesus!

No doubt they sent friends out to watch for him, to run to the house with news that he had been spotted, that he was on the way. And as Lazarus became less and less responsive, slipping inexorably toward death, they themselves searched the horizon in anguished frustration for a sign that Jesus was at least concerned about their plight. But there was no sign.

If they received any news at all, it was that the One to whom they had turned in the hour of their most critical need "stayed where he was for the next two days and made no move to go to them" (John 11:6). What terrible bewilderment they must have experienced! Frustration and bitterness evolving from a sense of betrayal would have been understandable. With each passing hour Mary and Martha's time-stress became heavier and heavier. Finally, it was too late— Lazarus had died. Time had run out.

Schedules: A Matter of Life and Death. Each of us has experienced time-stress when things don't go according to our schedule. God is gracious in that few of us experience the life-and-death stress faced by Mary and Martha, but we still run the full gamut of emotions when we have an important schedule, and time-stress is faced. Will the mortgage loan be approved before the interest rates change? Will we meet the deadline for completion and submission of the bid? Will the agreement be reached, the sale closed, or the contract signed on schedule? And time-stress takes its toll. Nervous anxiety. Unspoken desperation. Vexing frustration. Fear, even. All destructive manifestations of distress resulting from poorly managed time-stress.

Yet, in today's fast-paced world of schedules, deadlines, and quotas, how do we manage time-stress when things don't go as we think they need to?

The first step we must take is to realize that, once we have committed our lives to the sovereign control of God, it's impossible to experience time-stress over our schedules. Why? Because our schedule isn't really ours—it's *God's*. It's his schedule, his time, his plan. And it's all for his purpose and glory, and our good.

God's schedule concerns our eternal life. All things go according to his schedule—even in the case of Lazarus. Of course Jesus understood the desperate plea in the sisters' message! Of course he was aware of their anguish and he knew how their frustration would mount when he didn't appear in what they felt was a "reasonable" amount of time. He was fully aware that things wouldn't go, even remotely, according to what Mary and Martha and their friends believed was the necessary time-schedule.

But Jesus was on God's schedule, moving in accordance with God's purposes. So he delayed in responding. For two whole days! Far beyond what might be considered a "reasonable" or "explainable" delay. In fact, in view of the circumstances, Jesus' delay was incomprehensible. But notice what was uppermost in Jesus' mind: "The purpose of his [Lazarus'] illness is not death, but for the glory of God. I, the Son of God, will receive glory from this situation" (John 11:4).

Our schedules can never be "thrown off." They aren't *our* schedules. And the moment we accept this, and that God's schedule will always be perfectly timed to accomplish what he wills, that is when we will be able to manage the time-stress imposed by the demands of our days and involvements.

Too Many Activities, Too Little Time. Frustration and other feelings of distress often occur when it seems that there is too much to do and too little time available to do it. This stress is centuries old, as can be seen in the Book of Deuteronomy. Moses was overwhelmed with the enormity of the tasks he faced as the teacher, leader, judge, and administrator of his people. "You are a great burden for me to carry all by myself," he exclaimed to the people. "What can one man do to settle all your quarrels and problems?" (Deuteronomy 1:9-12). In response to this, Moses delegated responsibility to others.

The apostles, too, when faced with ever-increasing tasks, delegated responsibility (Acts 6:1-4). They established a guideline for time management, reflecting on the nature of their activities and deciding which ones their talents best suited. In other words, the apostles *prioritized.* They looked at the tasks which faced them, re-evaluated their primary goals; matched the time available and the tasks at hand; and concluded that they were detracting from their effectiveness by doing things they shouldn't.

The surest sign that a person needs to prioritize is when the "services" he has undertaken are causing him to be impatient and irritable, conveying to others that they are an inconvenience.

Procrastination: The Thief of Time. Make the most of your time, God's Word tells us in Colossians 4:5. And in Ephesians 5:15, 16, we are told to seize every opportunity we have to do good. There is never "a better time" to do something. The best time is now. Jesus' rebuke to a man who wanted to wait for a better time to accept Jesus' invitation to be his disciple proves that putting off important tasks is not acceptable (see Luke 9:59, 60).

"Don't waste time along the way," Jesus instructed his disciples in Luke 10:4 as he sent them out. He knew that time was to be respected, and used wisely. "All of us must quickly carry out the task assigned us by the One who sent me," he said in John 9:4, "for there is little time left before the night falls and all work comes to an end."

"If you wait for perfect conditions, you'll never get anything done." This wise observation from Ecclesiastes 11:4 is further proof that time should not be wasted.

Wait-time: The Stress of Delays. Four seconds. According to research, that's how long the average "wait-time" is. It's the amount of time a typical teacher waits for a student reponse before rephrasing his question or answering it himself. Four seconds! Hardly enough time to digest a question, let alone formulate a response. "Wait-time inadequacy," not being able to wait long enough for something, is one of the most difficult and important behaviors to change in a teacher.

Our fast-paced society, the demands of our roles, and the imperatives of our schedules create a tendency toward impatience. Nothing frustrates us as quickly as standing in line at the post office or store, or being stuck in a traffic jam, or caught behind a driver who seems to crawl for miles just when we're in a hurry to get somewhere.

If you doubt the distress of wait-time, analyze your reactions the next time you are delayed. You may be surprised—or even amused—by the emotional and physical responses you go through. Aggressive driving, horn-honking, shouting, obscene gestures, and muttered profanities are all distress responses to waiting.

Fortunately, the stress of wait-time is easy to manage. In fact, it can be a blessing! You can use wait-time as a time to pray—for people around you, for patience, for anything. When wait-time is regarded as a God-provided prayer time, another major step has been taken toward defusing the "time bomb."

Too Much Task: Too Little Time. Let's assume that the Scriptures have been adhered to, and that the following stress management steps have been taken relative to time-stress: Our schedule is relinquished—we work as hard as we can and leave the rest up to God; we follow the example of Moses and the apostles in prioritizing and delegating tasks; procrastination has become a thing of the past; and wait-time is regarded as a gift of prayer time.

But what if, despite following all of these scripturally derived stress management steps, we find ourselves faced with the stress of not having enough time to complete an important task. We have done everything possible, but we are faced with time-stress due to circumstances beyond our control. When this happens, there is one more step we need to take: analysis.

Through analysis we discover that, though circumstances are beyond our control, they are not beyond God's control. Therefore, we should abandon our often frantic efforts, and turn the situation over to the Lord.

"Listen to my words, for they are wise and filled with insight," the Psalmist beckoned in Psalm 49. "There is no need to fear when times of trouble come." And in Psalm 31:24, we read "Take courage if you are depending on the Lord." These words are strong encouragement in the face of plans that have gone awry. When we have done everything possible, the only way to manage the stress of too much task and too little time is to accept God's truth that "We can make our plans, but the final outcome is in God's hands" (Proverbs 16:1).

Summary
Time-stress and the Failure Phobia can be managed by following the examples in Scripture concerning the use of, and attitudes toward, time. We must study what God says about the true meaning of success, and understand that—for the Christian—there is no failure. And where there is no failure, there should be no fear of failure. We need to realize that our worth is immeasurable because of Jesus Christ; it does not depend on our accomplishments, or on how we use our time, but on Christ and what *he* has done. God, through Christ, has defused the time bomb, and released us from the Failure Phobia.

Twelve
Your Personal Prescription for Stress Management

Traveler's Advisory: Hazardous Roads Ahead
The windshield wipers thumped rhythmically in their valiant fight to keep clear a narrow arc of visibility. In the beam of the headlights and far beyond lay a vast and silent sea of billowing snow, broken only by the blurred outlines of dead spruce, which poked, mastlike, through the swirling blizzard.

Emil Matthes was totally oblivious to the storms; his years in the bush country of Ontario had virtually inured him to threatening weather. The leaden skies and rumbling cloud masses which emerged from the roiled and turbid expanses of Thunder Bay to the south or from the vast surface of Hudson Bay to the north generally evoked no emotion. They were just there. A fact of life.

But on this night, Emil felt anxiety. There was an uncomfortable emptiness in his gut. And he was perspiring, even though the frigid blasts of the storm sliced through the cab of his pickup and penetrated the insulation of his goosedown coveralls.

The report on the radio had been disjointed by static, but the gut-punching facts had spilled out: " . . . on an icy highway west of Winnipeg . . . critically injuring the driver . . . details were not available . . . at least one fatality . . . pending notification of next of kin. . . ."

How Emil knew it was his wife, Reta, he wasn't sure. After all, there was no reason why she should be on the road. Yes, she had planned to drive her mother and sister some seventy miles home following their holiday visit for Christmas, but Emil anticipated that they would stay at least a day or so longer to keep Reta company after his departure for the timber camp. Besides, the roads were slick, and although he, as the head of the timber cutting operation, couldn't delay in getting back to the bush country, there was no such urgency for Reta to go out. *Besides,* he told himself, *there are a half a million people in Winnipeg, I'm just being foolish.* But deep inside, he knew.

Within the hour, the deep treads of his truck's six-ply snow tires were churning back through their own half-filled ruts toward what would be the first of a series of stress-laden episodes for Emil and Reta Matthes. They would find themselves pushed to unanticipated depths of struggle, and to unexpected heights of faith.

The static-punctuated radio report had been at least partially accurate. Reta's sister and her mother had been killed. Reta would spend over seven pain-filled months in the hospital, and would carry with her for years the emotional and physical aftereffects of the accident. For Reta, the return to health would be agonizingly slow. (Over two decades later, her physical mobility is still restricted.) And Emil became responsible for emotionally bolstering Reta, caring for two young children, and managing a timber-cutting operation. Their odyssey through trials would be a long one. Emil and Reta Matthes were about to enter what Reta would later describe as "the most terrible time in our lives."

Vital Statistics: Vital Support. Other than the constant struggle through rehabilitative therapy, life for Emil and Reta, for the next four years after the accident, was relatively uneventful. The arduous monotony was broken by only one ironic highlight; Emil received an award for hauling one million cords of wood without an accident. He hardly had time to enjoy this recognition when trouble struck again: cancer. He was forty-two years old. And he had cancer.

"Low grade malignancy," the doctor said. But cancer, nevertheless. Growths on the bladder. They had to be removed. And they were removed. Continually. They were removed during fifty-three separate episodes of surgery, over a period of nine long years. They were finally removed for good through a urostomy—the total removal of Emil's bladder. That was 1972.

"We didn't know what would happen to us," Reta reminisced. "We were very upset, wondering how we would cope." And now it was 1985. "And now . . . now things are more devastating than ever."

Reta was describing their current agony. Emil had again, in late 1984, undergone major surgery so traumatic that he said later, "I felt that this time I would die. I knew, inside of me, that I had nothing left to fight with. But prayer pulled me through. Friends prayed. The people in my son's church prayed. Bible study groups prayed. And I prayed. All I asked for was strength. And then, too, people surrounded Reta and me with love."

When asked what advice they would give people to prepare them for the kinds of suffering they had experienced, Emil and Reta were unhesitating in their responses:

"Hold fast in faith. Tell people to be ready, and to hold fast to God's Word," Reta resolutely declared. "There is strength in God's Word. . . . In the midst of tribulation you will have the deepest communication with your God. You will know what it is to be able to fully talk to him."

"Remind them," Emil affirmed, "that God listens to all prayers." His voice was firm, stronger than it had been throughout the whole conversation. "All these troubles have brought us closer to God and have given us a greater understanding of faith in Christ. They have brought us closer together, too. Tell other Christians that in trying times, when everything goes wrong, not to give up. When things went wrong, I only prayed harder.

"And friends—their prayers and support—were of immeasurable help," he concluded.

Faith in God, prayer, the comfort of Scriptures, and the encouragement of friends were the supports that held Emil and Reta up as they traversed their "valley of the shadow of death."

As this book was being written, Emil Matthes was preparing to reassume his duties as Chairman of the Board of the Manitoba-Saskatchewan District of a major church body. Emil's ability to continue to dedicate himself to the service of others is the result of his personal program of guaranteed stress management. The specifics of his program follow.

The Latest Research: Three Thousand Years Old.
In the late eighteenth century, Sir Horace Walpole, the English author, coined a word whose light and tripping syllables were suggestive of the mood surrounding its meaning: *Serendipity*—the phenomenon of making accidental positive discoveries. The word would later prove to be of particular value to researchers, who would use its variants to describe discoveries that resulted from research for other things—much like the serendipitous discovery of America while searching for a passage to India.

One of the most delightful aspects of working in the field of Christian counseling is that, sooner or later, a scientific "discovery" validates what Scripture reveals—Serendipity. As the apostle Paul declared in Romans

3:4, "God's words will always prove true and right, no matter who questions them."

The serendipitous discoveries of the most up-to-date research provide proof for the skeptics of one clear fact: Perfect insight and perfect foresight for managing stress have been available for years! Nowhere is this more clear than in the field of stress management.

How Tough Are You?: Your "Hardiness Quotient." What are your personal chances of managing stress well enough that additional stress won't follow? For example, Baseball U.S.A.'s Doug Bliss managed his stress so well that he avoided the subsequent stresses of headaches, bitterness, resentment, sleeplessness, or any other similar condition. He was proof of what stress researchers in the last decades of the twentieth century had finally verified: It is not what happens to you that can result in further stress, but how you *manage* what happens to you.

The evidence that how you manage stress is more important than the stress itself in determining whether additional stress will occur is substantial and impressive. Dr. Paul Rosch, the president of the American Institute of Stress, hypothesized a plausible relationship between the incidence and pathology of cancer, and the personality traits a person brought to bear in coping with stress. Dr. Rosch implied affirmative responses to questions concerning stress and cancer:

"Can stress cause cancer? Do emotional factors play a significant role in accelerating the rate of malignant growth or in promoting metastases? Alternatively, is it possible that other emotions—a strong religious faith, an intense will to live, or even an aggressive attitude—can cause tumors to regress or actually to disappear?"[1]

Other researchers were even more specific. In 1984, following eight years of extensive study, two researchers at the University of Chicago, Drs. Suzanne Kobasa and Salvatore Maddi, reported that the most critical difference between people who became ill under stress and those who remained healthy was a set of personality traits. Kobasa and Maddi called these traits "hardiness" and said that these personality traits were executives' most potent protection against stress.

The stress-buffering power of *character*, "protected all classes of people," they elaborated, including women from all socioeconomic strata—U.S. army officers, blue-collar workers, management level personnel, and college students.[2]

"We now know," the authors of the report concluded, "that the way you handle [stressful] events dramatically affects your chances of staying healthy." In response to this conclusion, they developed a "Hardiness Test," and they are in the process of developing a program for teaching hardiness, or, to use their own terminology, for teaching or developing "character" and "inner resources."

How well you might manage stress, then, is determined by how "hardy" you are. And how hardy you are is related to your character or inner resources. Let's take a closer look at exactly what this means.

Hardiness: What Exactly Is It? Beyond calling hardiness a set of personality traits, or declaring that it had something to do with inner resources and character, the definition of this term was nebulous. Three factors were identified, however, as associated with hardiness: *Commitment* to self, family, and other important values; a sense of personal *control* over one's life; and the ability to see change in one's life as a *challenge* or opportunity to overcome.

The authors of the report described the behavior of a "hardy" manager who has had a fight with his boss:

"He'd come to work eager to resolve their differences. Deep involvement in his work, awareness of his strengths, and interest in all aspects of the company . . . could help him handle conflict . . ."

Hardy people also "accept support from their families and coworkers, and use that support well." In addition, the authors assert, even people who are in the dangerous, hard-driving Type A category may get rid of hostility and the drive of external pressure by feeling friendly and in control of their lives.

How Do I Acquire Hardiness?
Before outlining how the researchers suggest we acquire hardiness, let's consider again what they found:

1. How well you manage stress is more important than the stress itself in determining whether you suffer further distress.
2. Certain individuals who are "hardy"—who have character or inner resources—have proven able to avoid illness or other distress resulting from an initial stress.
3. Hardy individuals possess three main personality traits—commitment to something, a sense of control over life, and the ability to see life as a challenge.

The following guidelines from the authors of this hardiness research were first published in *American Health* magazine (Volume Three, Number Three, September 1984), in an article entitled the "Three Paths to Hardiness":

"In working with groups of executives . . . we have found three techniques help them become happier, healthier, and hardier. Though the techniques may work best in a group, you can try them on your own.

"Focusing. A technique developed by the psychologist Eugene Gendlin, focusing is a way of recognizing signals from the body that somthing is wrong. Many executives are so used to pressure in the temples, neck tightness, or stomach knots that they stop noticing they have these problems, or that they worsen under stress. We've found that it helps them to take a strain inventory once a day, to check out where things are not feeling quite right. Then they mentally review the situations that might be stressful. (We encourage group members to ask themselves questions like: 'What's keeping me from feeling terrific today?') This focusing increases your sense of control over stress, and puts you psychologically in a better position to change.

"Reconstructing stressful situations. Think about a recent episode of distress, then write down three ways it could have gone better and three ways it could have gone worse. If you have trouble thinking of what you could have done differently, focus on someone you know who handles stress well and what he or she would have done. It's important to realize that things did not go as badly as they could have—and even more important to realize that you can think of ways to cope better.

"Compensating through self-improvement. Sometimes you come face-to-face with stress, like illness or impending divorce, that you cannot avoid. It's important to distinguish between what you can and cannot control. But when life feels out of control, you can regain your grip by taking on a new challenge. Choosing a new task to master, like learning how to swim or tutoring a foreign student in English, can reassure you that you still can cope."

Stress, Science, and Scripture. When we study the scriptural guidelines regarding stress management, we make an amazing discovery: Centuries before today's researchers were even born, the Scriptures revealed the importance of strength of character and inner resources!

"Don't be conceited, sure of your own wisdom. Instead, trust and reverence the Lord, and turn your back on evil; when you do that, then you will be given renewed health and vitality" (Proverbs 3:7-8).

"All who listen to my instructions and follow them are wise, like a man who builds his house on solid rock. Though the rain comes in torrents, and the floods rise and the storm winds beat against his house, it won't collapse, for it is built on a rock.

"But those who hear my instructions and ignore them are foolish, like a man who builds his house on sand. For when the rains and floods come, and storm winds beat against his house, it will fall with a mighty crash" (Matthew 7:24-27).

Many other references speak of the inner resources that are ours through God's instructions and commandments. Once again, scientific research "discovered" what Scriptures revealed: Character and inner resources are keys to successful stress management.

But how are these "inner resources" or hardiness qualities attained? Again, Scripture provides the method. Steps for developing peace of mind and inner strength are listed at the end of Chapter 2. These same steps from God's Word can be followed to develop character and inner resources.

The Scriptures also address the three specific personal qualities that were mentioned earlier which researchers assert are indispensable to developing psychological hardiness.

First, a *commitment* to important values. Such a sense of commitment is not only attainable, but impossible to escape, once a person commits his life to Jesus Christ! He becomes committed to proclaiming the Gospel of Jesus Christ, and following the admonition of the apostle in Colossians 3:17: "And whatever you do or say, let it be as a representative of the Lord Jesus." A Christian has a total sense of purpose in life.

Second, Scriptures address a sense of personal *control* over one's life. The Christian who has turned his life and will over to Christ truly "loses his life to save it." He knows that he *retains* perfect control by *relinquishing* control to God, since his steps will be free of self-destructive error. "Trust the Lord completely; don't ever trust yourself. In everything you do, put God first, and he will direct you and crown your efforts with success" (Proverbs 3:5-6).

Third, we find scriptural help in developing an ability to see change in life as a *challenge*. The apostle Paul endured more externally imposed circumstantial stress than most people would suffer in two lifetimes. But he regarded every circumstance, including those filled with adversity, as an opportunity. "For to me," he declared with unshakable optimism, "living means opportunities for Christ . . . I have learned the secret of contentment in every situation . . . for I can do everything God asks me to with the help of Christ, who gives me the strength and power" (Philippians 1:21; 4:12, 13).

Comparing Research and Revelation
Let's go back for a minute to the researcher's suggestions on developing hardiness.

Research says that your sense of control over stress will be increased by *focusing,* or asking questions like: "What's keeping me from feeling terrific today?"

Scripture, however, provides the sense of control by telling us: "Don't worry about anything, instead, pray about everything; tell God your needs and don't forget

to thank him for his answers. If you do this, you will
experience God's peace, which is far more wonderful
than the human mind can understand. His peace will
keep your thoughts and your hearts quiet and at rest
as you trust in Christ Jesus" (Philippians 4:6-7).

Which method do you think would help you most
effectively deal with stress? Research or revelation?

Research suggests it's helpful to *reconstruct*, or to
evaluate how you handled a stressful situation and how
an admired role model might have handled it, thereby
finding better ways to cope. Scripture advises us to
pattern our lives after Jesus Christ, and gives account of
people who successfully encountered stress. In fact,
they "won battles, overthrew kingdoms . . . were kept
from harm . . . escaped death . . . [and] made whole
armies turn and run away" (Hebrews 11:33, 34). The
Scriptures provide a constant blueprint for the best
ways to handle stress-inducing situations.

Which way would you choose? Emulating a role
model who may have nothing in common with you and
searching within yourself for better ways to cope, or
emulating Jesus, the perfect role model, and following
specifically laid out instructions for coping?

Finally, research tells us that when things do, in fact,
reach the point of being out of control, you can
compensate, or "regain your grip" by taking on a new
challenge, such as learning how to swim or tutoring a
foreign student, to reassure you that you still can cope.
But consider deciding to tutor a foreign student in
English or learning to swim when you are faced with
the serious illness of your child or the imminent loss of
your job. Would you gain a greater capacity to manage
stress through such tasks, or through heeding the
scriptural advice to "pray without ceasing," and to "call
for the help of the elders of the church," letting your
spiritual family help you carry your burden? The advice

of research, particularly in this case, sounds uninspiringly empty.

Which would you choose, research or revelation?

Facing Stress with Relaxation. Other experts in stress management have offered additional methods of managing stress. For example, "The Relaxation Response," a method of reducing tension, was the title of a 1975 best-seller by Dr. Herbert Benson, of Harvard Medical School. It's also the phrase used to describe a method of dispelling, through meditation, the distressing effects of anxiety. The key to the success of Dr. Benson's method, which includes sitting quietly in a relaxed position, calls for the selection of a phrase or a prayer to focus on, one "rooted in your beliefs," that you can say silently while you exhale normally. For Christians, Dr. Benson advocates short Scriptures, such as "My peace I give unto you" (John 14:27, KJV), or "I am the way, the truth, and the life" (John 14:6, KJV).

Think about Dr. Benson's technique for a minute. It was popular enough to generate a best-seller. It was simple, and it worked. It led him to the belief that faith can help healing, and that "meditation based on heartfelt belief is not a discovery of (the new field) of behavioral medicine: It is old-fashioned prayer."[3]

Now think a little deeper, past Dr. Benson's suggestions and the new field of behavioral medicine. Think past the acceptance of Dr. Benson's methods by millions of Americans. Think back to the millennia-old insight outlined in the Scriptures:

1. "And you must think constantly about these commandments I am giving you today. You must teach them to your children and talk about them when you are at home or out for a walk; at bedtime and the first thing in the morning. Tie them on your finger, wear them on your forehead, and write them on the

doorposts of your house!" (Deuteronomy 6:6-7)

Millions who failed to heed God's wisdom in Deuteronomy, flocked to follow Dr. Benson's advice to meditate.

2. "Fix your thoughts on what is true and good and right. Think about things that are pure and lovely, and dwell on the fine, good things in others. Think about all you can praise God for and be glad about" (Philippians 4:8).

Millions who failed to heed this scriptural instruction, were thrilled by Dr. Benson's suggestion to pick out and repeat a word or phrase rooted in their beliefs.

3. Think back over everything God says about prayer, including the admonition to pray at all times. Millions who ignored the wisdom of God followed the "wisdom" of Dr. Benson's "discovery" that meditation is old-fashioned prayer.

Coincidence or confirmation? Research or revelation? Is it really surprising that Dr. Benson's relaxation response technique appealed to millions, and that it worked? It is merely a reflection of the wisdom of God, wisdom which has been available for thousands of years to reward those who "diligently seek him"; wisdom that produces, in the words of Jesus, "a gift—peace of mind and heart!"

Hardiness: What It Really Is
The photographer committed an act of foolish audacity, but he got what he wanted. He knew that, to capture the "presence" exuded by Winston Churchill—the "presence" that lifted the morale of the British people—he would have to resort to drastic measures. So he did just that. Just before his shutter opened to record the portrait of the inspirational wartime leader, photographer Yousuf Karsh yanked Churchill's

omnipresent cigar from the startled prime minister's mouth. And he got exactly what he wanted: A picture that showed the very essence of determined and pugnacious tenacity. This quality characterized the indomitable spirit of the British people throughout the ferocious assault on London during World War II . . . and was personified in the prime minister.

The portrait is now famous, for it recorded not only the visual likeness of Winston Churchill, but it captured something much deeper, something that Churchill and a select few others possess. Karsh could not ask the prime minister to "look this way" or to "look that way," because although he knew what he wanted to capture, he did not know how to define it. But, though the quality of "presence" could not be defined, for someone with insight, it could be captured.

So it is with the quality of hardiness. Though it cannot be accurately defined, it is identifiable. The qualities which accompany hardiness are implicitly understood; personal fortitude, strength of an inner origin, indomitability of spirit, and spirituality.

Certainly the quality of hardiness was dynamically operational in the lives of Emil and Reta Matthes. Just as certainly, the quality of hardiness was dynamically operational in the lives of: Cliff and Wilma Derksen, whose daughter was abducted and killed; Jim and Gloria Matthews, who continue to search for their abducted daughter, Jonelle; and Kennie Andersen, who survived financial crisis and emerged with unconquerable optimism.

In fact, the quality of hardiness is evident in the life of each triumphant person whose story is recorded in this book. But what did these stress-triumphant people have in common? Their personal testimonies provide a ready answer, and lead to several inescapable conclusions:

1. Whatever future research might finally say "hardiness" is, it is obvious that each of the stress-triumphant people in this book possessed this quality.
2. It is equally obvious that hardiness is a rock-solid attribute of the spiritual person. Further, while it might be possible to be hardy without being spiritual, it's not possible to be spiritual without being hardy. Therefore, to be spiritual is to be hardy.
3. Researchers, by their own admission, are seeking *perfect* methods to teach hardiness. Yet, methods for teaching spirituality or nurturing spiritual growth abound in Scripture. In other words, the Bible already has a course in "Hardiness Development" laid out for us!
4. Since a spiritual person must possess hardiness, it follows that the best way to develop the qualities necessary for managing stress is to develop the spirit. *The greater the spiritual commitment to living a Christ-centered life, the greater the capacity to manage stress.*

Mike Scott, the Matheses, Steve Smart, and the other victorious people in this book were paramount examples of people who lived Christ-centered lives. But what, specifically, did they have in common? Each of these people testified that they had total faith in the sovereignty of God; a total commitment to serving Christ; a steadfast belief that God provides the best for them; perseverance in seeking God's help; and an intense desire to know God through his Word.

These common characteristics are the keys to how we can develop the ability to say, with the apostle Paul: "I have learned the secret of contentment in every situation, whether it be a full stomach or hunger, plenty or want; for I can do everything God asks me to with the help of Christ who gives me the strength and power" (Philippians 4:12, 13). These characteristics are the keys to guaranteed stress management.

Creating Your Stress-Triumphant Personality

The preceding chapters in this book have presented, from the Scriptures, specific God-given instructions for coping with and managing *specific* kinds of stresses. But not only does God provide us with precise guidelines that are problem-specific; he has given us the wisdom to develop, nurture, and maintain a totally stress-triumphant personality. We turn now to what this book is all about: following God's guidelines for developing a stress-triumphant personality.

Step One: *Immerse Yourself in the Word.*

"I will never lay aside your laws, for you have used them to restore my joy and health. . . . Nothing is perfect except your words. Oh, how I love them. I think about them all day long. They make me wiser than my enemies, because they are my constant guide. Yes, wiser than my teachers, for I am ever thinking of your rules. They make me even wiser than the aged. . . .

"Your words are a flashlight to light the path ahead of me, and keep me from stumbling" (Psalm 119:93, 96-100, 105).

"For the reverence and fear of God are basic to all wisdom. Knowing God results in every other kind of understanding" (Proverbs 9:10).

"The knowledge of the Holy One is insight" (Proverbs 9:10, RSV).

"My people are destroyed because they don't know me" (Hosea 4:6).

"Jesus replied, 'Your trouble is that you don't know the

Scriptures, and don't know the power of God'" (Mark 12:24).

"So then faith comes by hearing, and hearing by the Word of God" (Romans 10:17, NKJV).

"So we must listen very carefully to the truths we have heard, or we may drift away from them" (Hebrews 2:1).

The Word of God testifies again and again, that a stress-triumphant life is available to anyone who will "consider the wonderful truth of the prophets' words" (2 Peter 1:19). Spiritual growth must and will occur for the person who asks God for wisdom (James 1:5), and who diligently seeks God in his Word. The Word of God, when studied, will always have an effect! (See Isaiah 55:11.) So Step One—immerse yourself in God's Word—in and of itself will lead to insight into the remaining steps, and will provide the dynamic catalyst for diligently pursuing those steps.

Step Two: *Memorize the Scriptures.*

"Keep these thoughts ever in mind; let them penetrate deep within your heart, for they will mean real life for you, and radiant health" (Proverbs 4:21).

"Talk with each other much about the Lord, quoting psalms and hymns" (Ephesians 5:19).

"I want to remind you that your strength must come from the Lord's mighty power within you" (Ephesians 6:17).

"Remember what Christ taught and let his words enrich your lives and make you wise; teach them to each other" (Colossians 3:16).

Many emotions, such as anxiety, fear, or guilt, can both result from stress and create more stress. But we don't have to go through this process! God gives us Scriptures to help us manage each potentially damaging emotion we face.

How might Judas Iscariot, for example, have handled the devastating remorse that must have seared the very core of his soul had he had available Paul's exonerative declaration, "Who dares accuse us whom God has chosen for his own? Will God? No! He is the one who has forgiven us and given us right standing with himself. Who then will condemn us? Will Christ? No! For he is the one who died for us and came back to life again for us and is sitting at the place of highest honor next to God, pleading for us there in heaven" (Romans 8:33, 34).

What might have happened to Judas if he had been able to drive away his self-recriminations with the Word of God? Suppose, instead of deciding he was beyond redemption, he had recalled with faith the words of the Psalms: "Though sins fill our hearts, you forgive them all" (Psalm 65:3), and "He is merciful and tender toward those who don't deserve it" (Psalm 103:8). Or suppose Judas had memorized the words of Christ when Jesus admonished Peter to forgive a transgressor "seventy times seven" (Matthew 18:22).

Consider the value placed upon memorized Scripture by a man whose ability to argue and persuade was a model of the art of "persuasive rhetoric."

The man had found himself at the bottom of the status hierarchy in a group of ship's passengers. He was a prisoner in transit, on board with military officers and conscripted soliders, merchants and traders, and experienced seamen as tough and unyielding as saltwater taffy. The crew had been battling a howling storm for days. In desperation, they had tossed cargo overboard and they had fortified the battered and creaking hull, which threatened at any moment to splinter into pieces at the next crashing assault of a tempest-maddened wave. Actions based on years of experience were of no avail; the hostile seas, driven by the relentless gale, continued to batter the ship. And now the basic survival instincts of the crew took over; prudence dictated that the lifeboats be lowered and the ship be abandoned.

Scarcely had the mainboat splashed into the fury of the sea when the terrified crew, as if abandoning their senses, cut it loose. They stared in desperation as their last hope of survival was swallowed into the swirling darkness.

What had driven them to this seeming madness? The persuasive powers of the man with whom this story began! This man, a prisoner, was able to persuade military men, naval officers, and calloused sailors to suspend their frantic activites and take time . . . to eat! He raised the crushed spirits of two hundred and seventy-six terrified souls, convinced them to stay together, and to deny rationality by setting the mainboat adrift.

Have you identified the man? The apostle Paul! The rest of this story, including the account of the sinking of the ship and the survival of its passengers, can be found in Acts 27.

Paul knew the necessity of supporting his teachings and arguments with quotations from the Scriptures. Repeatedly, throughout his letters, we find Paul saying; "As it says in the Scriptures," and "That is what is meant by the Scriptures, which say . . . ," and "For God says. . . ." Indeed, in one of his most important letters, Paul introduces his appeal with: "In the words of the Scripture . . ." He proceeds to use God's Word to create an irrefutable argument on the futility of work-based righteousness (Galatians 3).

The memorized Word of God was Paul's mainstay in his life and ministry. For each of the people in this book, it was the memorized Word of God that confronted and conquered the stresses of uncertainty, anxiety, illness, tragedy, and despair.

Step Two—memorizing the Scripture—will become

a reservoir of living water to quench the fires of conscience, cool the heat of conflict and adversity, and nourish the growth of a victorious spirit.

Step Three: *Fellowship with Other Christians.*

"Let us not neglect our church meetings, as some people do, but encourage and warn each other, especially now that the day of his coming back again is drawing near" (Hebrews 10:25).

"So encourage each other to build each other up, just as you are already doing" (1 Thessalonians 5:11).

One log, left by itself, may smolder. It may even, from time to time, dance into flame for a brief moment. Two logs will give off a brighter flame than one, and three a brighter flame than two. This applies to Christians as well. Christians who associate with other Christians are strengthened in their faith; they shine more brightly, they uplift and support one another. From the very beginning of time, God said, "It isn't good for man to be alone; I will make a companion for him, a helper suited to his needs" (Genesis 2:18). God's people have derived strength and encouragement from being with one another.

In every major city in the free world, Christian women and men can find Christian singles groups, Christian businesswomen's and businessmen's groups, Christian parents' groups, and other support or "help" groups and study groups, in addition to traditional church services. If you can't find such a group in your area—start one! The Lord himself promises: "Wherever two or three are gathered together in my name, there am I in the midst of them" (Matthew 18:20, KJV).

Christian fellowhip is vital when one is faced with problems and stress. Paul exhorts the Philippian Christians, "Is there any such thing as Christians

cheering each other up? Do you love me enough to
want to help me? Does it mean anything to you that we
are brothers in the Lord, sharing the same Spirit? Are
your hearts tender and sympathetic at all? Then make
me truly happy by . . . working together" (Philippians
2:1).

It was this type of caring fellowship that carried
Colonel Farrell Hupp, comptroller of NATO during the
Eisenhower administration, through the darkest days of
his life.

Colonel Hupp was a man intimately acquainted with
stress. In 1958, while stationed in Paris, he was
responsible for a budget of five hundred million dollars
a month. His jurisdiction extended from the United
Kingdom to North Africa. In addition to his duties as
NATO comptroller, he was also a United States
Treasury agent who had, and used, a direct access code
to the President of the United States. The demands of
his dual assignment subjected Colonel Hupp to
tremendous stress; stress he managed, but not well.

Various problems that carried possible international
repercussions made his life, in Hupp's own words, "a
living hell." He was not a committed Christian, but he
did develop coping mechanisms. Hupp suffered from
sleeplessness, forgetfulness, paranoia, intermittent
deafness, and splitting headaches—but he survived.

Over a decade later, he faced a second major crisis in
his life when the doctors told him that his wife would
be dead of a brain tumor within thirty days unless she
submitted to immediate neurosurgery. "The stress was
even worse," Hupp recalled. But by this time, he had
found some real stress-combatting resources—he had
accepted Jesus Christ, and had the support and love of
fellow Christians.

This time there were no headaches, no intermittent
deafness; no acute manifestations of distress. Because
this time Hupp had the support of the men in his

Wednesday Breakfast Bible Study Group. Farrell tells of his support systems and the power of Christian fellowship:

"The men talked with me and encouraged me. They prayed for me and with me, and they visited us. I looked forward to Wednesday morning like a little kid. Sometimes no words were said, but I could literally *feel* the effect of these spiritual people."

I joined Farrell at one of the Wednesday morning meetings. We sat quietly in the predawn darkness, hushed spectators to the faint rose-colored glow that seemed to emerge, almost imperceptibly, from deep within the massive drifts of the snow-capped Rockies. It was strangely peaceful in the "Wednesday Group room," located on the top floor of the Anaconda Towers in downtown Denver. Both of us, only a half hour before, had been a part of the stream of headlights far below, winding its way in to the heart of the city. We had each tolerated a long drive, the early hour, and the congestion of winter traffic in the city to be a part of this fellowship.

"What I told you before," Farrell said, breaking the silence, "about the strength I received—that's why I've committed myself to *never* miss this Bible study."

The significant strength one receives from the support of people who care is borne out by research. Heart attack patients who were socially isolated and who had a high degree of life stress, had more than four times the risk of death compared to patients with lower levels of stress and isolation.[3]

Fellowship—a major step toward stress management. A step that God has guaranteed to bless with his own presence.

Step Four: *Pray.* Remember the story from Mark 6 of the feeding of the five thousand? The apostles had just returned from the evangelizing tour which Jesus had sent them on. They had been telling him, in great detail and at some length, all that had been done by them, including what they had said. Jesus suggested they try to get away from the crowds to rest, so they left by boat for a quieter spot. But the crowds had gone on ahead, and throngs of people were milling about when Jesus and the disciples reached what was to have been a quiet, deserted place. Jesus ended up teaching until late afternoon.

Jesus then realized they needed to feed the people. He seated them in groups, blessed the food, distributed it to his disciples, talked again while everyone ate, and supervised the gathering of the leftovers.

Finally, Jesus gave his disciples further instructions, sent them off across the water, and remained behind to say good-bye to the crowds and supervise their departure.

Now, look again at some details: Jesus was tired and hungry early on as he listened to his disciples. So tired, in fact, that he tried to get away to an isolated spot for rest. Instead, he ended up working hard until early evening. By this time he was probably bone-weary, hot, and emotionally and physically exhausted. He ignored the hot sun, the demands of the crowds, the long hours of toil, teaching, and ministering, and then took on the additional task of seeing that everyone was safely on his way home.

Now, at last, it would seem Jesus could lie down on the soft warm ground, and allow the last lingering fingers of sunlight to relax him. Finally his bone-penetrating fatigue could be dispelled by the rest he had sought early in the day. But the Scriptures tell us something we do not expect; "Afterwards he went up into the hills to pray!" (Mark 6:46). And he must have prayed at length, for we are next told that "during the night" he saw that the disciples were in trouble.

Jesus knew the source of his power. In the Gospel of

Luke, Chapter 5, we are told, "But he often withdrew to the wilderness for prayer" (v. 16). In Luke 6:12, it says, "He went out into the mountains to pray, and prayed all night!" If the Gospels are read with a focus on Jesus' prayer life, it is astounding to discover how he constantly sought opportunities to pray.

It has been said that Martin Luther spent at least two hours at the beginning of each day in prayer, except on days when he had an extremely taxing and time-consuming work load. On such days, he spent three hours in prayer!

A popular cliché states, "Prayer changes people— people change things." But that is not what God says. God, in his Word, says that prayer can direct the course of men and of nations, that the person who loves God should pray constantly, that one must pray without giving up, that our persistence in prayer is noticed by God, and that he will respond to all our prayers. Prayer is so significant, so vital and indispensible to our strength and our well-being, that "the Holy Spirit helps us with our daily problems and in our praying. For we don't even know what we should pray for, nor how to pray as we should; but the Holy Spirit prays for us with such feeling that it cannot be expressed in words" (Romans 8:26).

Step Four—prayer—is an irresistible offense in confronting stress, and an impregnable defense in resisting distress.

Step Five: *Serve Others and Obey God.* Almost every Christian knows another Christian who seems to have endless energy. This person is always working, always helping, and always joyful and optimistic. It's almost as though his service to others leads to a positive outlook and to an assertive boldness in meeting and surmounting problems.

That's exactly what God promises us when we obey

his commandments and serve others. The Scriptures about service and obedience read like a list of gifts of stress-conquering powers. Service and obedience help us know the deep values of life. In Mark 8:35, Jesus describes the confidence of knowing what life is all about: "If you insist on saving your life, you will lose it. Only those who throw away their lives for my sake and for the sake of the Good News will ever know what it means to really live."

Service and obedience constitute a path to God's blessings, which include peace, joy, patience, fearlessness, and confidence. After washing his disciples' feet, Jesus said: "You know these things; now do them. That is the path of blessing" (John 13:17).

Service to others strengthens one's own faith. And greater faith leads to greater service. The capacity to walk with God is ever-increasing.

Step Six: *Guard the Temple.* Assault. Rape. Murder. These are a few of the "subjects" majored in by Linda Glick's students. They shuffle into her classroom each day, chained at the ankles with escape-preventive shackles. Sullenness, rebellion, profanity, functional illiteracy, emotional problems, and an achievement gap among her students (who range in age from twelve to seventeen years old and who are the lowest functioning students in the state of Colorado) generate constant stress for this twenty-seven-year-old teacher who works for the state department of correctional institutions.

When asked how she managed this stress, Linda didn't hesitate for even a second. "I made sure I got plenty of rest," she said. "I *never* went to work tired. And I exercised faithfully, to be certain that I was in top physical condition."

That was it. No biofeedback, no spontaneous autohypnosis, no ninety-second relaxation technique. Linda Glick simply met the stress-inducing demands of her job by being as well-rested and physically fit as she could be.

This same insight was offered by two competing Christian businessmen in response to the question: "What would you add as an important step in God's program of stress management?" Each man manages stress quite well. Lee Yoder owns a GMC auto dealership that employs close to one hundred people; his friend Herrick Garnsey owns a Ford agency, a mere glance away, that provides income for almost as many employees. Both men have a deep respect for the truth in the verse, "Know ye not that ye are the temple of God, and that the Spirit of God dwelleth in you?" (1 Corinthians 3:16, KJV).

"Stay physically fit," Herrick Garnsey advises. He knows that if one is physically run-down, even minor stressors become major problems. Exercise and fitness, Garnsey asserts, hone the edge, giving one an extra sharpness in cutting through problems.

And the other side of the coin is etched by Lee Yoder, who advises rest. "The Scriptures say that the Sabbath was made for man. I make it a point not to work on the Sabbath. It's a natural day for worship and for the family. If we do what God says, and set aside one day for him, we'll have better family relationships." Yoder, who regularly puts in eleven hour days, six days a week, and whose energies are freely expended in helping others after work hours, interrupted our conversation to respond to an employee's problem. The interruption dealt with, he turned back to me. "If you keep the Sabbath," he said, sharing what was obviously a deeply held conviction, "you'll be better able, all the way around, to deal with your job during the week."

You can accomplish Step Six by doing only those things on the Sabbath which are not a regular part of the "work" you do for a living. "Work" at chopping wood (unless you are a woodcutter) or playing golf (unless you are a golf pro). Guard the temple by honoring the Lord's injunction to set aside a day—a day he declared "was made for you!" Guard the temple with moderation in all things (Philippians 4:5, KJV), and in the God-sanctioned pursuit of physcial fitness.

Guard the temple—your physical body—with adequate rest and sound health maintenance.

Step Seven: *Make a Total Commitment.* Seven—the number symbolizing completion. Step Seven, perhaps, should have been the first step in God's guaranteed program of stress management, for when a total commitment is made every other step flows freely.

Total commitment was exemplified by Jesus; he is the perfect role model. Commitment to his Father's will dominated his life. Every word, action, and reaction was a declaration of total commitment. Though faced with a horrible and painful death, Jesus "moved steadily onward toward Jerusalem with an iron will" (Luke 9:51).

The reasons for total commitment are inescapable. They both impel and compel, for deep within the heart is an awareness of our need, as outlined in Scripture, to yield ourselves to God's plan for us.

"Where is the man who fears the Lord? God will teach him how to choose the best. He shall live within God's circle of blessing, and his children shall inherit the earth" (Psalm 25:12, 13).

"The steps of good men are directed by the Lord. He delights in each step they take" (Psalm 37:23).

"And if you leave God's paths and go astray, you will hear a Voice behind you say, 'No, this is the way; walk here'" (Isaiah 30:21).

"Blessed be the name of God forever and ever, for he alone has all wisdom and all power. World events are under his control. He removes kings and sets others on

their thrones. He gives wise men their wisdom, and scholars their intelligence" (Daniel 2:20, 21).

"Our only power and success comes from God" (2 Corinthians 3:5).

"How well he understands us and knows what is best for us at all times" (Ephesians 1:8).

Step Seven—the completion step of total commitment.

The Full Circle: Scriptural Insights and Perfect Peace
We have now come full circle in developing a program of guaranteed, Scripture-based steps to stress management. Step Seven, total commitment, leads back to Step One, immersing yourself in God's Word. And Step One, through the inherent power of the Word and the sanctifying power of the Holy Spirit, ultimately leads back to Step Seven. This total commitment to God, the development of the spiritual man spoken of in 1 Corinthians 15:45-49 and 1 John 3:2, 3, leads to an insight that, by its very nature, will incorporate, as a way of life, each of the other steps of triumphant stress

management. In this way, we are empowered through Christ and the Holy Spirit to live a joyous, victorious, distress-free life.

"May the Lord of peace himself give you his peace no matter what happens. The Lord be with you all" (2 Thessalonians 3:16).

Endnotes

Foreword
1. George L. Engel, "A Life Setting Conducive to Illness: The Giving Up-Given Up Complex," *Annals of Internal Medicine* (1968), 69:293-300.
2. George L. Engel, "Sudden and Rapid Death During Psychological Stress: Folklore or Folk Wisdom?" *Annals of Internal Medicine* (1971), 74: 771-782.

Chapter Twelve: Your Personal Prescription for Stress Management
1. Paul J. Rosch, "Stress and Cancer," *Consultant* (November 1984), 73-76, 81-94.
2. Suzanne Quellette Kobasa, "How Much Stress Can You Survive?" *American Health*, 3, No. 6 (September 1984), 64-77.
3. William Ruberman, M.D., et al. "Psychosocial Influences on Mortality after Myocardial Infarction," *The New England Journal of Medicine*, 311 (August 30, 1984), 522.

Helpful Reading

Children

Burron, Arnold. *Discipline That Can't Fail: Fundamentals for Parents.* Milford: Mott Media, 1984.

Lewis, Paul. *Forty Ways to Teach Your Child Values.* Wheaton, Ill.: Tyndale House Publishers, Inc., 1985.

Ortlund, Ann. *Children Are Wet Cement.* Old Tappan, N.J.: Fleming H. Revell, 1981.

Marriage

Cooper, Darien. *You Can Be the Wife of a Happy Husband.* Wheaton, Ill.: Victor Books/Scripture Press, 1979.

Crab, Lawrence. *The Marriage Builder.* Grand Rapids: Zondervan Publishing House, 1982.

Frydenger, Tom and Adrienne. *The Blended Family.* Grand Rapids: Zondervan Publishing House, 1985.

Mumford, Amy Ross. *It Only Hurts Between Paydays.* Denver: Accent Books, 1979.

Sanford, John and Paula. *Restoring the Christian Family.* South Plainfield, N.J.: Bridge Publishing, Inc., 1979.

Williams, H. Page, and John D. Coleman. *Do Yourself a Favor: Love Your Wife.* South Plainfield, N.J.: Bridge Publishing, Inc., 1979.

Substance Abuse: Addiction

Drews, Toby Rice. *Getting Them Sober.* South Plainfield, N.J.: Bridge Publishing, Inc., 1980.

Dunn, Gerry G. *God Is for the Alcoholic.* Chicago: Moody Press, 1967.

Mehl, Duane. *You and the Alcoholic in Your Home.* Minneapolis: Augsburg Publishing House, 1979.

Straek, Jay. *Drugs and Drinking: What Every Teen and Parent Should Know.* Nashville: Thomas Nelson Publishers, 1985.